Streamlined Library Programming

STREAMLINED LIBRARY PROGRAMMING

How to Improve Services and Cut Costs

Daisy Porter-Reynolds

 LIBRARIES UNLIMITED

AN IMPRINT OF ABC-CLIO, LLC
Santa Barbara, California • Denver, Colorado • Oxford, England

Copyright 2014 by ABC-CLIO, LLC

All rights reserved. No part of this publication may be reproduced, stored in a
retrieval system, or transmitted, in any form or by any means, electronic, mechanical,
photocopying, recording, or otherwise, except for the inclusion of brief quotations in a
review, without prior permission in writing from the publisher.

Library of Congress Cataloging-in-Publication Data

Porter-Reynolds, Daisy.
   Streamlined library programming : how to improve services and
cut costs / Daisy Porter-Reynolds.
      pages cm
   Includes bibliographical references and index.
   ISBN 978-1-61069-408-7 (pbk.) — ISBN 978-1-61069-409-4 (ebook)
1. Libraries—Activity programs.   2. Public libraries—Centralization.   I. Title.
   Z716.33.P67   2014
   027.4—dc23   2013045194

ISBN: 978-1-61069-408-7
EISBN: 978-1-61069-409-4

18   17   16   15   14   1   2   3   4   5

This book is also available on the World Wide Web as an eBook.
Visit www.abc-clio.com for details.

Libraries Unlimited
An Imprint of ABC-CLIO, LLC

ABC-CLIO, LLC
130 Cremona Drive, P.O. Box 1911
Santa Barbara, California 93116-1911

This book is printed on acid-free paper ∞

Manufactured in the United States of America

To Leslie, Aleta, Birgit, Shirley, and Raelene

Contents

Preface

In 2010, as Manager of Innovation at San José Public Library (SJPL), I kicked off centralized programming at our municipal, general-funded 19-building library system. San José, the heart of Silicon Valley, is America's 10th-largest city with a population of just under a million. Thirty-eight percent of residents were born outside the United States, and 55 percent speak a language other than English at home. This level of ethnic diversity makes library programming a complex and fascinating endeavor. We began centralization at a time when we expected our budget to be slashed, and it was; several months into the new model, our staffing and therefore branch open hours were reduced by 17 percent. Yet we were delivering 25 percent more programs than we had under the old model.

My year of implementation was many things—rewarding, frustrating, eye-opening, exhausting, stressful, fun—but it was never boring or easy. Without a book like this to follow, I charted my own course, navigating around and through hazards such as employee buy-in, union pushback, stakeholder panic, understaffing, pay cuts, and an ever-dwindling budget. The handful of other library systems who have taken this path faced different sets of barriers. The issues you face at your own library will be different, but it's my hope that this book will help you work through them.

Acknowledgments

Special thanks go to Leslie Tanaka, Aleta Dimas, Raelene Velarde, Birgit Vogler, and Shirley Tanase, my central unit at San José Public Library, without whom centralized programming would never have happened. Maddy Walton-Hadlock, Sharon Fung, and Pam Crider were strong supporters on the front lines. Jane Light dreamed up the idea and was an inspiring mentor. Angie Miraflor and Kary Bloom made me laugh despite all the stress. Brooke Ballard, Janis O'Driscoll, Christina Stoll, Amy Mather, Cindy Mares, and Donna Gecsaman provided perspectives from other libraries. Boyd Porter-Reynolds was and is, in this as in everything, my cheerleader. Thank you all.

If you're from a one-building library, a complete centralized programming approach might not work for you, but you can still reap many of the benefits associated with it. This is where the word "streamlined" comes in. Many of the concepts described in this book can be easily adapted to your single building, such as efficient marketing, storytime boxes with interchangeable elements, and the administrative development of program priorities.

This book is a comprehensive guide to getting started with centralized programming or infusing some of its principles and strategies to improve your current programs—helping you work more efficiently as you improve the quality of your programs. It's directed primarily at public libraries of all sizes, but could also be adapted to other agencies that focus on programs, such as park districts or some special libraries. The book draws on my experience as the centralized programming lead at a large urban library system, as well as from interviews with other librarians across the country who have successfully streamlined their programming services.

Have you already decided centralized programming is for your library? If so, think of this book as a map to walk you through the steps you need to succeed at this complex task. Centralized programming is a relatively recent concept, but those libraries who have already begun will, via this book, share their best practices and tips on how to avoid some potential pitfalls. It walks you through the essential steps, including the decision about whether and how much to centralize; getting buy-in from stakeholders; choosing a project team; how to staff the workgroup; the types of programs you might offer and how to develop them; the logistics of program selection and delivery; and evaluation and continuous improvement to make sure you stay on top of your game.

If you're still deciding whether to centralize programming at your library, here are some questions to consider:

- Are you facing budget cuts, reduced hours, or layoffs? Would you like to emphasize direct customer service over backroom planning?
- How much staff time does it take to offer programming at your library system? Include preparation, marketing, setup, delivery, cleanup, and evaluation. Where do you see opportunities for efficiency?
- What other costs are involved in programming at your system and how would centralization lower them? For example, does each branch order supplies separately, taking up staff hours as well as resulting in extra shipping costs and no bulk discounts? Does each branch have a closetful of puppets that are only used once or twice a year and take up valuable storage space? Does each location create and print its own monthly program brochures or calendars, writing their own promotional descriptions for programs?
- Is your programming of consistently high quality among locations? For example, does one location have a great computer class teacher but isn't as

strong on storytime? Does a branch have knitting clubs several times a week but no book discussion group and no staff with the expertise to lead one?

- Does your library's vision statement or strategic plan include specific programming priorities? Do you find it difficult to apply these consistently across your system? Or does each location currently set its own priorities for programs?

- Have you tried centralization of other library services—collection development or IT, for example? Have you gained efficiency while improving quality and consistency, or did you find it was better to select materials and repair computers locally at each branch? If you have centralized some processes, did it go smoothly or are you still working out the kinks? How did staff react?

There are no right or wrong answers to the above questions, but discussing them at a management or librarian meeting may help you decide whether now is the time for you to proceed with streamlined programming. You don't have to do it all at once! Maybe this year, you'd like to begin by ordering supplies centrally, or creating a few storytime boxes. Maybe your library isn't quite ready for that, but you're facing staff cuts, and need to reduce the number of programs you offer while still meeting the community's needs. Maybe you have a terrific storyteller at one branch and you think she could exchange some hours with a nearby location to maximize the quality of what they offer while still ensuring coverage at her branch. Taking these steps toward quality improvement and efficiency will have immediate effect and also lay the foundation for future streamlining plans.

If you're ready to get started, turn the page and let's begin with a scan of your current environment.

Getting Started

Congratulations! You've made the decision—it's time for you to streamline your library's programming. Let's get started.

WHERE YOU ARE

Forget the adage, "You've got to start somewhere." Actually, it's more specific than that: you've got to start from where you are. Worksheet 1.1 can help you take stock of what your library is currently doing programming-wise before you decide where you want to go.

At San José Public Library (SJPL), we made a few calculations. We figured out that across our 19 locations, we'd presented 2,604 programs in the fourth quarter of 2009. This included 466 unique programs, some of which were repeated many times (e.g., the Teen Advisory Board met monthly at each branch). Just over half of our programs were recurring in this way, with another 40 percent being one-time programs. Nine percent were already centralized to some degree; either they were part of a system-wide effort, such as summer reading activities, or else, they were delivered by a cluster of collaborating branches.

We surveyed librarians throughout our system and learned that the average full-time librarian spent 26 hours per month planning and marketing programs, and only 13 hours actually presenting them. Considering that most recurring programs were happening at every branch—for example, we were offering a preschool storytime at least once per week at every location—we could see that there was a lot of redundancy built into this model. If staff at 19 locations each spent one hour per week planning and marketing the storytime and one hour delivering it, that adds up to 152 librarian hours per month spent on this task system-wide. If we could figure out how to do the marketing and promotion centrally, leaving the presentation to the individual branches, this number could drop dramatically. Like so

WORKSHEET:
GETTING STARTED, TAKING STOCK

Use this worksheet as a planning tool at your earliest streamlining sessions.

1. How many programs does your library deliver each year?

   _____

2. How many locations (departments, branches, outreach sites) do you serve with programs?

   _____

3. What is the total attendance at all programs over the last year?

   _____

4. How many of your total programs are duplicates (e.g., preschool storytime was offered 102 times; introduction to email was offered seven times)?

   _____

5. To which audiences are you delivering programming? Adults, children, teens, seniors? Job-seekers, retirees, parents? Readers, reluctant readers, pre-readers? At-risk teenagers, first-time home-buyers, elementary-school teachers? List any groups to which you have specifically targeted programs.

   _____

   _____

6. How much is your programming budget? How is it divided? Is this revisited every budget cycle or has it remained the same for many years?

   _____

   _____

Worksheet 1.1   Getting Started, Taking Stock. © San José Public Library

From *Streamlined Library Programming: How to Improve Services and Cut Costs* by Daisy Porter-Reynolds. Santa Barbara, CA: Libraries Unlimited. Copyright © 2014.

many other libraries in early 2010, we were facing budget cuts that would mean layoffs and reductions in service hours, and this efficiency seemed not only ideal, but critical.

WHERE YOU WANT TO GO

Now that you have a good idea of where your library is, you can figure out where you want to go. Which of the following does your library already have?

- a library mission or vision statement, or a strategic plan
- a programming vision or priorities
- target audiences for programming

If your library has already thought through its programming goals, terrific—you're ahead of the game. If not, now is the time to begin. Here's how a few public libraries went about doing this:

- Arapahoe (CO) Library District had two objectives in its library-wide strategic plan: Empowerment through Literacy and Building Community Connections. When planning programming, they decided to simply use the same objectives—focusing on storytime, adult literacy classes, and book discussions as well as developing a network of community resources.
- Arlington Heights (IL) Memorial Library created vision and values statements to formally capture the impact of the library's presence in the community. Based on these, they set four priorities for the next year, including a focus on high-profile programming as well as the development of two key audiences: teens and the business community. Programming decisions were made with reference to these priorities.
- Santa Cruz (CA) Public Library convened a task force on financially sustainable service models. Their final report recommended focusing programming efforts on youth literacy, high-impact adult events, and community-generated programs by local experts.
- SJPL based its programming priorities on the 2007 United Way Silicon Valley Community Impact Report. Rather than reinventing the wheel, they relied on the detailed surveys and analysis of the community's needs that United Way had already completed. This resulted in six priorities for library programming: Reading Promotion, Cultural Traditions & Life Enrichment, Effective Parenting, Physical & Emotional Well-Being, Services to New Americans, and Support for Formal Education. When the 2009 update to the United Way report came out, the library built on the work already done in 2007 to create SJPL's Educational Priorities:

If you're truly starting from scratch, take a hint from Brett W. Lear, author of *Adult Programs in the Library* (Lear, 2013, 55–59). Lear recommends beginning by building a community profile. This document will help

SAN JOSÉ PUBLIC LIBRARY:
EDUCATIONAL PRIORITIES

Literacy

Info lit, reading promotion, ESL, media literacy, tech skills, adult literacy, test prep, support for formal education, FLCs

*Storytime * Conversation Club * Intro to Facebook * Homework Center * Math Fun * Silicon Valley Reads * Mad Science*

Culture

Arts, crafts, gardening, cultural traditions, world culture, languages, cross-cultural understanding

*Lunar New Year * Teen Crafts * Posada * Making Musical Instruments * Vietnamese Singing * Knitting Circle * Drummm*

Community

Civic engagement, citizenship, voter registration, environmental issues, volunteerism

*Citizenship Q&A * teensReach * Councilmember Office Hours * Greening Your Home * Disaster Preparation * Friends Meeting*

Health

Wellness, health literacy, physical education, nutrition, exercise

*Snack Smart * Vietnamese Health Database * Tooth Time Storytime * Health Info Online * Diabetes Prevention * Wii Tournament*

Parenting

Child development, school readiness, early literacy, child safety

*Reading Readiness * Toddler Time * Mother Goose Storytime * Parenting Workshops * Puppet-Making for Families*

Finance

Jobs, careers, business, money management, retirement planning, economic self-sufficiency, consumer awareness

*Job Hunters Support Group * Before You Buy * Find a Job Online * Foreclosure Prevention * Get Your Annual Credit Report*

Figure 1.1 Educational Priorities for San José Public Library (2010). © San José Public Library

you figure out who your customers are and how you can tailor programs to suit them. For example, does your city have a large number of senior citizens, or single parents, or job seekers, or English-language learners? Acquiring and analyzing this data will help you advocate for these groups, target your marketing, and justify your budget and priorities. While the creation of a community profile is beyond the scope of this book, Lear suggests two titles you can read to get you started:

- *Planning for Results: A Public Library Transformation Process* (1998), Ethel Himmel
- *Planning Library Programs* (1979), Petty O'Donnell and Patsy Read

Once you have a community profile, the rest of the process becomes a lot easier.

HOW TO GET THERE

Take a look at your existing programming. If you're like most public library systems, it will vary dramatically by branch—as it should. Unless your service area is completely homogenous demographically, you will want to tailor programming to the specific communities in which you'll offer it.

Unfortunately, too often, the inconsistencies in programming are random rather than strategic. If you have a librarian at one branch who loves to knit, that branch will have a knitting club, while the branch across town with plenty of seniors and high circulation of needlecraft books might have none. Or a branch one block from a high school doesn't do much teen programming because no one at the branch feels qualified to deal with this age group. Or storytimes at one location are so popular that they've had to restrict attendance just because that branch doesn't have a meeting room and the children's area is tiny.

There are other solutions to these problems, such as reallocation of staff or holding programs before the branch opens to the public. But one of the best strategies is to centralize or streamline programming. This way, a central team can look at the big picture and work with the branch staff to think about programming from the customer's point of view. If one branch needs a knitting club, but no staff have the requisite interest or skill, then that's a problem to solve, not a need to ignore. Seek out a volunteer to run the club, perhaps in conjunction with a staff member who doesn't know how to knit, but is willing to learn, and has the energy and enthusiasm to handle the club logistics. Or arrange a staff trade with someone from a branch with an avid knitter. Every Tuesday evening, say, the knitter runs a knitting club at branch X, which in turn sends a staffer to cover the desk at the knitter's branch.

If you're at a large, multibranch library, consider designing a set of core programs. For example, at SJPL, we decided on a set of core programming that every location would offer. Each branch would provide the following:

- Two, three, or four storytimes per week, depending on the size of the branch
- A weekly Conversation Club, drop-in casual practice for English-language learners
- A monthly Teen Advisory Board meeting
- Various seasonal programming, such as a Back-to-School Night

Some branches argued that their teens weren't the joining type, or that they didn't have the staffing to do three storytimes, but the central team insisted that they at least make the effort. And they did. In most cases, the branches were surprised to learn that the statement "if we offer it, they will come" proved true. However, in a few cases, it became clear that, for example, Branch Z was located in a neighborhood without many new English speakers and that one to two customers per Conversation Club did not make for good conversation!

In addition to the core programs, you may also choose to set a target number of additional, custom programs for each branch. This is what we did at SJPL. We needed to do this because of the differences in program ideology among the branches. There were a few that were used to doing multiple programs every day, and they needed to be reined in, to focus on quality over quantity and not compete with themselves. There were also a few who had decided that programming was not a core service and that no one would come anyway; we worked with these branches to show that if they offered targeted programming and marketed it effectively, customers really would come in, and that this would also boost their circulation statistics.

In a large and heterogeneous city such as San José, it didn't make any sense for us to assign each branch a specific number of programs in each of our Program Priority categories (see Fig. 1). The neighborhoods were so different, and the branch staff so knowledgeable about their local communities, that it made more sense to let each branch manager set local standards. This also meant that the branches had the freedom to try out different types of programming to see what worked best, and focus on different priorities at different times of the year (cultural programming around the holidays, for example). However, your own library system may be different. Work with branch managers to determine needs and then act accordingly.

If, on the other hand, you're at a smaller library and are streamlining rather than centralizing, you might consider determining specific numbers or percentages of programs that will address each of your priorities. If reaching out to English-language learners is a goal for your library, you could decide that 15 percent of programs should be offered in a language other than English, or that 10 percent of your programming should address needs such as citizenship test preparation or English conversation practice. Or you might want to say that 20 percent of programs will be offered in conjunction with the park district, or in partnership with the school district, or be presented by local talent. It's up to you what goals you'd like to set and how specific you'd like to be.

In conclusion, streamlining or centralizing will save your library both money and time. By combining big-picture thinking with local talent and experience, you can improve quality while actually reducing costs. Remember, your mileage may vary! There are 8,951 public libraries in the United States (IMLS, 2013, 96), which means there are 8,951 ways to streamline programming. You will need to tailor your strategies to your local community and your existing staff. Proceed to Chapter 2 for advice on managing this important change.

2

Change Management

Are you sold on the concept of streamlined programming? Terrific—but many of your staff won't be as enthusiastic. Centralizing and streamlining programming can be a particularly difficult change for branch librarians and managers. After all, they're the ones who know their communities, and they've been in charge of program planning for years. They're used to designing their own programs from scratch, on their own schedule, and tailored to their own skills. Who are we to come in and start telling them what to do?

Some of the negative feedback you might hear during your transition to centralized or streamlined programming includes the following:

- You don't know my community, so you can't plan for my branch.
- You're trying to make all the branches cookie-cutter and get rid of what makes us unique.
- I didn't go to library school so I could have a job playing video games with kids.
- I don't have the time to learn everything in this program box.
- My librarians don't feel any ownership over programs now.
- Our Friends group won't stand for this.
- No one in my neighborhood would care about a program like that.
- If you won't let me plan programming, what am I supposed to do all day?
- Teen programs don't work at this branch.
- You just sit at headquarters in your ivory tower and decide what I should do in a neighborhood you know nothing about.
- You're taking away all my creativity.

Do these statements sound familiar to you? They're normal reactions to change in a library system—any change at all. There has always been, and will always be, a perceived disconnect between headquarters and branches, whether the industry is libraries, banking, retail, or any other. There is no quick solution, but two-way communication helps tremendously. Knowing what reactions to expect from your branches and planning to include them in the implementation of streamlined programming will help in alleviating growing pains.

CHANGE MANAGEMENT BASICS

There are hundreds of books about change management, and dozens specifically for libraries. But here, in a few words, are the basics:

1. Listen to your staff.
2. You cannot overcommunicate.
3. Don't wait for everyone to be on board.
4. This too shall pass.

Listen to Your Staff

One of the reasons staff resent top-down change is that they don't feel heard, respected, or empowered. They believe that the people making decisions are too detached from the front lines to understand the ramifications. Is this fair? Sometimes. We've all met administrators who have no idea what the customer wants, or who make decisions based on their own preferences rather than paying attention to customer data. So don't be that person! Listen to your frontline staff. They know a lot about the library. You have the big picture, yes, but they have the details, and both are crucial to successful implementation of any change.

Involve frontline staff in your implementation process early and often. Just because they don't have a say in *whether* to centralize programming functions doesn't mean they can't contribute good information about *how* to do it. For example, they probably have a better sense than administrators do about the best days and times to schedule programs for different audiences. They may be the right ones to put together storytime boxes, since they read to little ones every week. They might have input on the best month to kick off centralization or streamlining efforts, based on vacation patterns or school holidays. And you might get some of the best information from someone who's the most vociferously opposed to centralized programming. It's important not to discount someone's opinions about details just because they disagree with you on the big picture.

You Cannot Overcommunicate

Maybe you could, but it would be pretty hard to do so. The fact is that some people want to bury their heads in the sand, particularly about stressful changes that will affect their jobs. Presenting at a staff meeting isn't enough; for a change as grand as complete centralization of programming, you'll want to be on the agenda at every staff meeting for several months, repeating the basics and adding or changing new information as you have it. In February, you might say that the library is looking at ways to streamline—such as centralizing programming—and explain what that means. At this point, asking for information and ideas from staff will encourage buy-in during these early days, and you'll be able to tell who's already on board. In March, you might be able to call for volunteers for your work team. In April, that work team might present some broad strokes about your action plan. In May, maybe you'll be able to say that you expect the first month of full centralization to be January. Even with all this advance preparation, a lot of staff members might be shocked by May's news; often, it isn't real until there is a date attached, even though they've been hearing it for several months now.

In addition to communicating often, communicate using several methods. Speaking in person at meetings is effective, of course, so that you can take questions and gauge reactions. But follow up with email correspondence so that those slower on the uptake, or those who missed the meeting, can react and ask questions as well. Showing written documents and plans can also help show that you know what you're doing and have thought through the consequences, as there will always be some staff who believe you're acting on a whim or following a trend without thinking it through. And after implementation, as you're starting out, create a way for staff to provide feedback on specific programs or presenters. (You'll read more about this in Chapter 10.)

Don't Wait for Everyone to Be on Board

Really, don't, because you'll wait forever. There will always be staff who are completely resistant, who will never agree with centralizing or with any other change to the status quo, and who just want everything to be the way it was when they started working for your library in 1992. You must, of course, give the message plenty of time to sink in; you don't want to email announcing you're moving to a new programming model, starting in a week! But don't fall into the trap of waiting for everyone to get used to the idea before you get started. Pick a timeline that allows for a lot of planning and revision, and stick to it as best you can.

This Too Shall Pass

Change results in angst, no question about it. The angst will subside with time—more time than you'd like, in many cases—but it will subside. Think back to other changes you've made throughout the years. Has your system centralized collection development? Remember the outrage? How many people still talk now about the good old days when they got to select books for their branches or departments? A few, maybe, but overall most people aren't thinking about going back to those days. They may even be wondering how they had time for selection with all the rest of the tasks they have to do now.

Even if your library system hasn't done any centralization or other systemic change, think of how your staff have reacted to other kinds of changes. A new director, a new bookmobile route, discontinuing one of the book clubs, weeding the VHS tapes . . . the staff were likely upset about these changes too, but eventually they got over it. This too shall pass.

For another take on how to gain staff support for implementing changes in programming, see Chapter 2 of Jennifer Nelson and Keith Braafladt's *Technology and Literacy* (2012, 16–18). Nelson and Braafladt list 11 strategies that they've found useful [reprinted with permission]:

- Know your organization: Figure out who your stakeholders are as well as who really makes decisions—not necessarily just the top of your organizational chart.

- Build relationships thoughtfully: Now that you've identified the key people, how can you support each other throughout the tumult of organizational change?

- Prepare a program outline and timeline: It's important to pay attention to details and be able to predict where you'll be at a given time, but don't let over-analysis delay your project.

- Ask colleagues you respect to review your plan: The more feedback you get, the stronger your plan will be, which builds credibility for the project.

- Talk about your project early and often: No one should be blindsided. It takes time to adapt to change, so be sure to build that into your timeline.

- Be prepared to compromise: The big picture might stay mostly the same, but the details definitely won't. Be flexible where you can, and remember you don't have all the answers.

- Know the details: Be confident about your plan before you roll it out, even though you know it will be adjusted along the way. If staff have a question you can't answer, let them know you'll figure it out and get back to them.

- Don't waste time: Run efficient, effective meetings and stick to the topic. Have action items to be completed before the next meeting and stick to your timeline.

- Be smart about deadlines: Hold everyone accountable for both short- and long-term due dates, and be sure to communicate changes in expectations.

- Demonstrate your idea to anyone and everyone: Be transparent about what you're doing and be ready to show examples to your staff and to show success stories from other libraries.

- Use laptops if possible: This final strategy is the only one of Nelson and Braafladt's 11 that applies only to individual programs, not to the big-picture changes discussed in this book. Their point is to be flexible and turn any space into a learning space.

THE TRAFFIC LIGHT MODEL

A classic theory of change management (Pritchett, 1996, 3–4) states that about 20 percent of your staff will look forward to the new way of doing business. Thirty percent will dig in their heels and say it'll never work. The remaining 50 percent will be skeptical but open-minded; they want to see it in action before they make a decision. A good shorthand for these three types of staff are Green, Red, and Yellow, similar to the corresponding traffic lights.

Red staff are often your most senior employees. They've been around longer than you, so obviously they know what will work and what won't work. They know that service trends come and go and that this is just a flash in the pan, this silly centralization concept. Yet, if you can get past the initial grumpiness, Red staff often have a lot to offer to streamlined programming. Their years of frontline experience have given them a ton of institutional knowledge about your library and your community. Take advantage of this!

Greens tend to be newer employees: librarians fresh out of school, recent transfers from other libraries, or paraprofessionals new to libraries. They have not been entrenched in the traditional system long enough to feel too much ownership of it. Or, they've worked in another library that's different from yours but still performs well, so they know the power of fresh perspectives. If they're recent library-school graduates, they may feel that they're on the cutting edge of library innovation due to studying a variety of service models. Working with Greens is refreshing because they're eager and willing, but it can be frustrating as well if your Green staff is too new to have a deep understanding of your community. Greens may also be easily discouraged by Reds, and they may not understand the importance of their contributions.

Yellow staff are a mixed bag; after all, they're half of your employees. They're open to change, but suspicious of fixing what may not seem to be broken. They may feel that since customers come to storytime, it must be working; sure, we could try some improvement, but let's wait and see how it goes before we commit. This is a perfectly reasonable attitude, and this is why Yellows can be a mellowing influence on the Greens and an inspiring one to the Reds.

In the next chapter, we'll talk about building your project team. You will want a mix of Green, Yellow, and Red staff because they all have plenty to offer. Getting your Red staff on board will mean teaming them up with Green staff, but also with the Yellow staff; Reds might dismiss the Greens as naïve or too new to the field to understand just why things won't work, but they may listen to the Yellows.

CHANGE MANAGEMENT: LIBRARIANS

Librarians can be a tough sell when it comes to centralizing their traditional responsibilities. I knew when we started planning the programming model at San José Public Library (SJPL) that the perceived loss of creativity and local control would be difficult for branch librarians to face. Indeed, some librarians were in tears, and some were enraged. Many others, of course, were eager to try the new model, but this was not the majority opinion.

One contributing factor to the angst librarians felt was that at the same time we were working on centralized programming, the City of San José was facing a huge budget crisis. Hundreds of city workers had been laid off, including many library staff. Branch libraries were reduced to four days of service per week. This was obviously a high-stress time as staff worried about their own job prospects, and even those with enough seniority to avoid the layoffs faced the loss of their longtime colleagues and dealt with survivor guilt. Plus, all staff faced potential redeployment to different assignments in order to maximize the manpower we had left.

Knowing that uncertainty about the future was stress-inducing and wanting to help alleviate that, our project team created a PowerPoint presentation about what a branch librarian's duties would look like after programming was fully centralized. It was presented at a librarian meeting by librarians, not managers or administrators, and it helped librarians understand what they would be doing if not developing programs: providing direct public service, promoting programs and services via social media and outreach, weeding local collections, training and supervising volunteers, coordinating after-school homework help, maintaining community contacts, and more. All of that would be in addition to the programming duties branch librarians would still carry out: suggesting programs to the central team, selecting programs from the monthly menus, hosting or delivering programs, and evaluating them afterward.

If you sense stress and anxiety among your staff members, consider scheduling time to outline the program in further detail, answer questions, and combat misconceptions and fears. Whether this is presented with Power-Point slides or with other tools is up to you, and will depend, among other things, on how many staff will attend. Just don't let it devolve into a gripe session—be clear about the purpose of the meeting from the start. This isn't a question of "if," but of "how."

The other piece of our presentation was the rationale. It was important that we not be seen as jumping onto a trend or sacrificing customer service in the name of efficiency—two things that frontline staff often accuse the administration of doing. We wanted to point out that, instead, this was a well-thought-out solution that would provide consistent quality of programs in addition to the natural efficiencies gained. We showed some statistics we'd gathered to determine exactly how much time is spent every week duplicating a preschool storytime at 19 locations, for example. And we said over and over that the programs in boxes we'd present would be created by SJPL librarians, not by outside consultants or retailers. This helped the librarians to see that we did, in fact, respect and rely on their expertise.

Amy Mather of Omaha Public Library (OPL) says that her team also struggled with the question of centralizing programming without harming the creativity and innovation of branch programmers used to creating their own events. Their solution? They encouraged local programmers to create programs that could be easily adapted to other branches, and even provided an online space (KitKeeper, in the case of OPL) for program instructions and supply lists (Amy Mather, email message to author, April 6, 2013). This is a great way to boost morale while also harvesting the experience and skill of your branch librarians.

However, this can encourage underground local program planning, so make sure you have checks in place to ensure that staff are complying with the big picture. For example, you can ask branch or department staff to check with you before spending the time developing programs and only add preapproved ones to your menus. Or, you could analyze (or have someone analyze) any gaps in your programming based on your program priorities and request that local staff create only programs that meet this specific need. You could even divide up program-creation responsibilities among your departments or branches to make sure everyone has the chance to shine in this role.

CHANGE MANAGEMENT: BRANCH MANAGERS

Branch and department managers can be some of the most challenging stakeholders to work with on the streamlining or centralization of programs. They're used to having complete local control over their building, staff, and customers. Some of them will feel threatened by a central team that suddenly has authority over programming, particularly if that team comprises their peers and staff rather than their superiors.

The key here is to see and treat the branch managers as experts. I don't mean to spin your relationship that way or to be disingenuous, but to actually believe it, because it's true. Branch managers can be a tremendous source of information and support for you as you implement centralized programming. They know their customers, and they know the strengths and limitations of their staff. The more branch managers you can involve in planning and implementation—especially the most influential ones—the better.

CHANGE MANAGEMENT: OTHER STAKEHOLDERS

Resistance to change can come from unexpected places. At SJPL, the centralization of programs faced opposition from not only staff, but from external stakeholders, primarily the Friends of the Library groups. Each of our 19 locations had its own Friends group, though the range of support varied along socioeconomic lines. Some Friends groups were large with many donors, while others were just a couple of enthusiastic people who had more time than money to donate to their branches. All were so passionate about libraries that they volunteered their own time toward fundraising. Obviously, they felt strongly invested in their local branches.

Because of the economic disparity among the branches, and because of the limited programming budget that city funds could provide, the wealthier half of the Friends groups funded almost all the programming at their own branches. This freed up the city funds to go to the branches without deep Friends pockets. However, this also meant that the Friends at the wealthier branches felt perhaps more invested than they would have otherwise in the programs offered at their locations and felt that they deserved to have some say in the program planning. They, like the staff, wanted the same library events they'd offered for years: say, the same magician every June and the same swing band every October. They were reluctant to accept a centralized model where the branches picked programs from a menu that didn't necessarily include local favorites. In a few cases, they did not want to write checks to the library to fund a particular program, preferring to pay the performer directly as they always had.

As with staff, the path to helping the Friends through this change begins with communication, communication, communication. Make a point to attend your Friends group meetings to explain the changes and how they will ultimately help the library. I attended meetings of the All-Friends group (representatives from each location's Friends who met quarterly) and of the Library Commission (the library's advisory board, who also attended Friends meetings). I passed out programming menus so they could see the number of options available, and explained that I'd be happy to consider their suggestions for future menus. I told them that the reason checks had to be written to the library rather than directly to the performer was because we got discounts for bulk purchases and their money would go further toward quality library programs. This was popular news. I talked about how efficiencies such as centralization translate into fiscal responsibility and careful stewardship of city and Friends dollars. I took their questions and quelled some myths that had arisen in the initial panic over the change. Did I completely convince everyone in the room that centralized programming was the way to go? No; the Friends fell into Red, Yellow, and Green groups, just like the staff. But it was a start.

Library staff and other stakeholders play a variety of critical roles in the implementation of streamlined and centralized programming. You'll need their help on big-picture thinking as well as local customer habits. The more you can do to create buy-in and smooth the path to change, the more successful your project will be.

3

Project Team

Now that you've scanned your environment, taken stock of where you are, and let your staff know what to expect, the next step is to select your project team and begin working on implementation of the project.

A NOTE ON TERMINOLOGY

In this book, when I refer to the "project team," I mean the group of staff who are planning centralized or streamlined programming. Usually, they have other primary assignments, but have also been asked to serve on this group. They are a planning team. At San José Public Library (SJPL), we called this group PDAT, for Program Development Advisory Team.

When I refer to the "central unit," I mean the staff you'll hire whose primary responsibility is to plan and deliver programs to your libraries. Their permanent jobs are as centralized programmers. At SJPL, we called this group UPS, for Unit for Programming Services. Other libraries have different strategies, as you'll learn later, such as age-based central teams or a decentralized team that meets regularly and reports to an administrator.

PROJECT TEAM CHARGE

Your project team will do most of the hard work from now until kick-off. They have the responsibility for designing how streamlined programming will work at your library, for creating an implementation plan, for convincing other staff to buy in, and for transitioning from decentralized to centralized programming. After kickoff, you'll still need a programming advisory team, which may or may not be the same group as your project team—that is entirely your choice. There are both pros and cons here: on the one hand, the original team believes strongly in your concept and has historical knowledge of what choices were made and why; on the other hand, your plans will necessarily change as you go forward, and it can be difficult for former project team members to let go and accept a modified model. Only *you* can decide which is right for your library.

One of the biggest charges of the project team is to develop job descriptions for the centralized programming unit. The team will figure out how many staff are needed, what qualifications they should have, and what their duties will be. (See Chapter 4 for a more detailed discussion on how to staff your central unit.) Depending on the structure of your organization, the team may also interview and select staff for transfer into the central unit, or they may turn that process over to the human resources department or to library administration.

The sooner you're able to bring the central unit's permanent staffing on board, the sooner they can get started with working toward implementation. In the meantime, the project team is responsible for this transition. They need to determine what kinds of programs will be offered at the start of implementation. They need to decide which branches need how many programs, and must then develop a menu of options. They also need to begin creation of the actual programs in boxes, and train staff on how to use them. They'll book paid performers and community partners to make presentations. They'll determine how annual event series such as the Summer Reading Program fit into centralization. They'll work with your board, Friends group, and other community stakeholders to help them understand the benefits of the model. And, of course, they'll spend time with the branch staff, easing them into the new model. They have their work cut out for them!

THE MAKEUP OF YOUR TEAM

For a project this large and sensitive, you need a strong and well-organized team. If you've already identified a manager for your central programming unit, you might consider her for the team leader, since she presumably has qualities such as enthusiasm, leadership, organization, and a zest for programming. If you haven't hired a manager yet, your team leader should be a Green staff member who is also a manager or administrator and has the respect of the organization—both upper management and front-line staff. You need a can-do person who runs meetings well, delegates effectively and fairly, and has the authority to assign action items and due dates. This can be someone who comes from another industry but is new to libraries, or who's new to this specific library, or who has worked in the library for several years, but isn't jaded yet.

For the rest of your team, create a good mix of Green, Yellow, and Red staff (see Chapter 2). You will need the energy and enthusiasm of the Greens, the organizational knowledge of the Reds, and the logic and reason of the Yellows. Be sure to diversify in other ways as well—staff from different branches and the main library, staff who work with children as well as with teens and adults, staff who have experience working with different demographic groups, and so on. At SJPL, we wanted to make sure to include teen, adult, and children's librarians. We wanted representation from the east side as well as the west side of the city. We wanted staff experienced with working with speakers of San José's four biggest language groups (English, Spanish, Mandarin, and Vietnamese). We wanted librarians from our headquarters, who tended to be specialists, as well as generalists from branches. We made sure to have a representative from a branch that offered family literacy services. And that's just the librarians! We also needed branch managers, an administrator to serve as advisor, and representatives from the marketing team and the volunteer office, since their roles were integral parts of the new programming model. Yet we didn't want a team of 20, because it's hard to get work done in a group that size. We ended up with a team of nine—larger than we'd originally envisioned, but also with enough people to accomplish the substantial amount of work that had to happen before kickoff.

Of course, your needs will vary depending on the size of your library and the scope of your project. If you're completely centralizing all of your programming, your group should be large, as SJPL's was, because you will want to make sure you've covered all your bases as far as representing various responsibilities and specialties. However, for a smaller library or one that's streamlining rather than fully centralizing, you may prefer a smaller team for efficiency's sake and to avoid pulling people away from front-line tasks. Or if your library is centralizing just a portion of its programs—for example, storytimes—your team will have a narrower focus and might include only youth services staff. In any of these cases, you'll still want someone with decision-making authority to attend the meetings and make sure the group's priorities are in alignment with the system goals.

In order to keep the project team fresh, be sure to specify terms of service on your call for interested staff. At SJPL, where our project team would also stay on as an advisory group, we decided that some of the team would serve two-year rotations and some would serve three. That way, not all of the current team's terms expired at once. We also determined that the four librarians permanently staffing the centralized programming unit would take turns attending, since if they all came to each meeting, it would mean quite a few hours taken away from their regular duties.

Treat this assignment just as you would a new job opportunity and a real commitment. For example, I sent out an email to all librarians and managers, seeking volunteers to serve on the project team and asking them to write back with their qualifications. I also asked for permission from applicants' supervisors, since the time commitment was significant and the workload would be heavy. Then, two administrators and I sat down with all the applications and we put together a team that attempted to cover all of the areas mentioned in the previous paragraph. We came pretty close!

TIMELINE

Your team's first responsibility will be to set up a timeline. Working backward from your projected kickoff date, what has to happen by when? For example, to figure out when you need to hire librarians for your central unit, refer to Table 3.1 (below).

The real fun comes when you start thinking beyond your kickoff date. Modifying the schedule to include October and November program planning and inverting it to a chronological order results in what you see in Table 3.2.

So, September 1, the big day when centralized programming kicks off . . . is also the day you'll be sending November program menus to your branches. This can be discombobulating. It's easy to think that the work will slow down after kickoff, but that's really not true. Your project team's work will diminish after you hire your central unit, but the newly-hired unit will have a ton of work to do—and all at the same time that they're designing and presenting programming for all of your locations! This is why it's a good idea to have your central unit in place at least three months before kickoff, and for your project team to finish as many transition tasks as they can in the meantime.

Table 3.1   Example of pre-kickoff timeline for centralized programming

Kickoff	September 1
Program boxes sent to branches by	August 20
Program calendars ready for branches by	August 15
Paid performers booked by	July 25
Staffing assignments for individual programs ready by	July 20
Branches make selections from menus by	July 15
Menus go out to branches by	July 1
Program array chosen by central staff by	June 25
Central staff hired by	June 1

Table 3.2   Example of comprehensive timeline for centralized programming

Central staff hired by	June 1
September program array chosen by central staff by	June 25
September program menus go out to branches by	July 1
Branches make selections from September menus by	July 15
Staffing assignments for individual Sept. programs ready by	July 20
September paid performers booked by	July 25
October program array chosen by central staff by	July 25
October program menus go out to branches by	August 1
September program calendars ready for branches by	August 15
Branches make selections from October menus by	August 15
September program boxes sent to branches by	August 20
Staffing assignments for individual Oct. programs ready by	August 20
October paid performers booked by	August 25
November program array chosen by central staff by	August 25
Kickoff	September 1
November program menus go out to branches by	September 1
Branches make selections from November menus by	September 15
October program calendars ready for branches by	September 15
Staffing assignments for individual Nov. programs ready by	September 20
October program boxes sent to branches by	September 20
November paid performers booked by	September 25
November program calendars ready for branches by	October 15
November program boxes sent to branches by	October 20

TRANSITION TASKS

Besides starting the actual day-to-day work of programming that the central unit will finish, there are many transitional tasks that your project team can and should accomplish before kickoff. Hiring the central unit is a big one, but there are plenty of others too.

Communicate, Communicate, Communicate

As discussed in Chapter 2, it's nearly impossible to over-communicate to staff about the pending changes. Representatives from the project team should attend every staff meeting they possibly can, and should be prepared to handle staff anxiety and anger professionally, calmly, and kindly. Present what you know at the time, and promise you'll come back the next month and share what's happened in the meantime. Leave plenty of time for questions.

It's easy to say, "expect negativity," but it's much harder to deal with it in the heat of the moment in a roomful of people. Here are some tips that may help in such instances:

- Whenever possible, provide more information rather than less, so that you appear (and are!) knowledgeable, transparent, and communicative. At the same time, when you're not sure of something, say so: "Good point, Kirk. We haven't yet worked out all of the details of routing the programs in a box among branches. I agree that it's unacceptable to rely on a truck that might break down, so we're going to think of solutions like getting the boxes out as early as possible or having backup plans in place."

- Acknowledge feelings without agreeing to change or cancel the project because of them, and offer options for participation: "I'm sorry you're upset, Roberta. It must be frustrating to think about not being able to choose your own storytime themes like you're used to. The best way to make an impact on the storytime boxes is to serve on the team that will create them. Look for an email about that in the next couple of weeks, and I hope you'll consider joining the relevant team."

- Remind staff that all of this will be tweaked as you go along, in both large and small ways: "You're right, Kevin, we're breaking some new ground here and it's hard to predict how our customers will react to having unfamiliar staff presenting programs. Customers are the reason why we're here at all, and we're going to do what we can to make sure these changes are seamless for them. We'll reevaluate along the way as we see how the customers react, so please send us an email if you have a suggestion."

If you're presenting at meetings that include groups of librarians, you can also get their input on programs they'd like to see. You could pass around sheets of paper and ask people to write down themes for storytime boxes and suggested books that match those themes. In addition to serving as a starting point for the boxes you'll build, this might help you get some names of people you'd like to serve on your storytime box development team.

Pick a Storytime Box Development Team

The best way to do this is to ask the question, "Who are our premiere storytime librarians?" There are probably several local experts among your staff. Just make sure that they aren't all Red or Green librarians; you need a healthy mix that includes all three colors as well as staff with different areas of expertise. Depending on the size of your library and how many boxes you'd like to create, this team should have four to eight members. More information about developing this group can be found in Chapter 5.

Survey Branches for Seasonal Programs and Favorites

The project team can use a free online survey program to seek feedback right from their desks. Ask the branch staff what their communities expect from them every year; maybe there's a big neighborhood block party at one branch each August and the library always has a storytime and craft booth. Maybe a certain local elementary school has Dinosaur Month in October, so the library tries to book some related programs at that time. Maybe Black History Month is critically important at one branch, but barely noticed at another, or perhaps it's Veterans' Day or Mexican Independence Day that's more relevant at another branch. You'll need to know this for the next step.

Create an Annual Program Plan

Once you have the survey results back, the project team can start to roughly sketch out the next year of programming at your library. This should be a 12-month year, so if you're kicking off on September 1, you want to plan through August 30 of the next year. This doesn't mean you have to know exactly what speaker you're having at 3:30 P.M. on a Wednesday 10 months from now; it does mean that you'll want to jot down that the Lunar New Year falls in early February this year, and so, that would be a good theme for programs at that time. This is just to get down the basics from your survey and your knowledge of local community calendars. Later, the central unit can flesh this out using *Chase's Calendar of Events* or a similar resource to figure out that July is National Ice Cream Month, and work that in, if necessary.

Allocate Your Budget

It's difficult to give advice on budgeting for streamlined programming simply because every library system is so different—not just in the dollar amount of the budget for programming, but in its structure (personnel vs. capital vs. operating costs, for example) and in its timing (how far in advance you must plan). Here are a few general tips to tackle this issue:

- To determine staffing levels for your central unit, calculate how many centrally-staffed programs you want to offer system-wide per week; then think about how many programs each librarian will be able to deliver. (This can vary based on your service area; a large county will have a lot more driving time between branches than in a smaller city.) If you think you want one staffed program at each location every week and you have 20 libraries, and you think a full-time librarian can deliver two programs per day, then you'll need two of them to meet this target. However, don't forget to leave time for all the other work these staff will do—creating box programs, planning for in-person programs, arranging paid performers and partners, training volunteers, attending meetings, and so on. In San José, we had 19 locations and one staffed program per week, and we had two full-time and two part-time librarians. It still was not enough.

- If you're making storytime boxes that will be routed along with your other branch deliveries, spend the money to get extremely durable ones. Cardboard isn't durable enough when the boxes are routed and used so frequently.

- Before purchasing central programming items such as a button-maker or a Wii, ask around at the branches to see if any library dollars have been spent on these at branches. Then, you can ask that these items be forwarded to your central team and sent out as box programs.

- Make sure each branch has some basic programming supplies, so you don't have to route as much for each box program. For example, at SJPL, we knew that every branch had just created a flannelboard as part of a grant project, so we were comfortable including a flannelboard set as part of each storytime box without having to deliver the flannelboards themselves. We also expected each branch to have crayons, construction paper, glue, and scissors, but we would include in boxes everything else needed for a specific craft, such as glitter, popsicle sticks, buttons, and so on.

- For paid performers, consider alternate funding before making allocations. As mentioned in Chapter 2, if some branches have generous Friends groups who will fund paid performers, then you can allocate more library money to the branches who do not.

Figure Out Your Menu Structure and Logistics

Here, your team will decide what will be the best way to present programming menus to each branch each month or quarter. Will you email the selections to the branches or upload them to your intranet? How will you get them back? What happens if a branch misses a deadline?

And what will the menu itself look like? In addition to programs and descriptions, it should include a grid indicating what priority the program serves and who is presenting the program (central staff, local staff, volunteer, partner, paid performer). This is a lot of information to juggle. There are some sample menus provided in Chapter 8, but yours may vary dramatically, based on local needs.

Assign Target Program Numbers

This can be one of the most difficult things for a branch manager or librarian to hear—that someone else is telling them how many programs to do. Some will feel insulted by the low number you assign them, saying that they're capable of so much more and that the community demands it. Others will say there's no way they have time to do all those programs, so you'd better give them more staff while you're at it. Either way, having the support of your administration is key here, so make sure the administrator on your team is comfortable with the numbers before you roll them out. The target numbers should be approved by the entire project team, including the administrative liaison, who can then advise you on the right route to get a signoff from other stakeholders.

Regardless of specifics, to get administrative buy-in, you will need to present a complete and detailed plan. Does your library have a leadership meeting you could attend to present your ideas? You might attend this to share your draft plan, while making certain you anticipate questions or concerns in advance so that you're ready with answers. Also, be sure to address specific support you will need. The example above is a good one—will you have backup from administration to enforce program target numbers? What else do you envision needing authority for—presentations to the board? Negotiation with vendors? This will vary, depending on your library's structure and on the scope of your plan, but be sure to think this question through and discuss it with administration.

How do you determine target numbers for programming? I asked Christina Stoll, program services manager at Arlington Heights Memorial Library (AHML), how she set targets. Her advice:

- Begin by scanning current numbers as well as past ones to see if there has been a trend of yearly increases or decreases in each department.
- Look at any existing directives or goals; for example, at AHML, there were priorities set to develop two specific audiences—teens and businesses—so these numbers would be higher.
- Communicate to managers and librarians why you're going to set targets (to avoid spreading audiences too thin, to prevent competition with other programs internally and externally, to make the best use of the budget).
- Write out some ballpark figures, then meet individually with each department to negotiate these.
- Get support from the administration before finalizing numbers.
- Continue to monitor and tweak, as circumstances require. (Christina Stoll, email message to author, June 4, 2013)

The tasks outlined on the previous pages should all be accomplished before implementation. As mentioned, you will also need an ongoing advisory team to ensure your model is working well and to respond to internal and external changes. This team may do some or all of the following:

- Develop annual work plans
- Monitor and tweak existing system priorities for programming

- Update target numbers
- Add to or subtract from mandatory programs
- Develop evaluation tools for measuring program success
- Allocate resources
- Monitor trends in programming and determine whether they're applicable for your community

Remember to include Red, Green, and Yellow staff in this advisory group. You can decide how much overlap its membership will have with your initial project team or even with your permanent unit staffing, which is discussed in the next chapter.

4

Staffing

Whether you're planning on full centralization of programming for your library system, or just centralizing the programs for a certain audience, such as children or Spanish speakers, you will need a team of dedicated staff. There are myriad ways to design such a team, and your local bud get policies and staffing strategies will determine the limits of what you can do.

CALCULATING STAFFING LEVELS

How many centralized staff you'll need depends on your program target numbers. If you have 20 locations and you'd like each of them to have one program per week for adults, one for teens, and one for children, that's 60 programs per week. If you're a single-building library with separate departments for children, teens, and adults, your numbers will look different. How many can each central librarian do? That too depends. If you're in the first scenario and want all of the programs to be presented by central staff, you're probably looking at three to five librarians. Let's look at the following figures:

60 programs per week,

divided by six days on which programs are offered = 10 programs per day.

If a librarian can do 3 programs per day, then you need 3.3 librarians,

but if a librarian can only do 2 programs per day (say, if you're in a large geographic area with plenty of travel time needed between stops), then you need 5 librarians.

And that's only taking presentation time into account. What about prep time? Promotion? Evaluation? Selection of future programs? Staff meetings?

Plus, keep in mind that scheduling can be challenging. You obviously can't do teen programs at noon on a Wednesday, at least, not during the school year. For kids' programs, your timing depends on whether they're school-aged or younger, but even for the little ones, you have to schedule programs around their naptimes. Adult programs shouldn't really happen between 9:00 A.M. and 5:00 P.M. on weekdays unless they're jobseeker programs or aimed at retirees or those with alternative work schedules, such as a homeschoolers' group or a Medicare online training session.

Let's try a different set of calculations. Again, you have 20 locations and you'd like one program for each age group per week. But this time, you'll limit programs presented by the central unit to one per week.

> 60 programs per week,
>
> in-person programs limited to 20 per week,
>
> divided by six days = 3.3 programs per day.
>
> If a librarian can do 3 programs per day, then you need 1–2 librarians.
>
> If a librarian can do 2 programs per day, then you need 2 librarians.

Again, that's just for the presentation part. You will still need other staff to plan and prep these programs as well as other programs you'll offer that will be locally staffed.

At San José Public Library, our central unit consisted of one part-time manager (that was me; I was full-time, but was also running our Innovation unit), two full-time librarians, two part-time librarians, and one full-time clerk. We made it work, more or less; however, we were constantly stressed out and never really caught our breath the whole first year. Based on my experience, I would recommend a full-time manager, two full-time clerks, three full-time librarians, and four part-timers for a library our size.

We had 19 locations and were committed to one centrally-presented program per week per location. We also required every location to have a weekly ESL (English as a Second Language) Conversation Club, two to four storytimes per week, and a monthly teen advisory board meeting. All of these were created centrally as programs in a box to be delivered locally. The Conversation Club was designed to be run by a volunteer if the branch had one available; a librarian with an interest in teen services generally ran the teen group; and, only librarians conducted storytime.

Early on, we'd divided our 19 locations into three groups: small, medium, and large branches. The main library was in the medium category, despite having by far the greatest square footage and circulation, because it had historically low program attendance figures. Based on these three categories, we set target numbers for programming. For example, a large branch might have the following monthly offerings:

- The required programming listed above
- Four centrally presented programs

- Six programs in a box
- Four paid programs
- Three volunteer-presented programs
- Various events by outside agencies, such as Friends of the Library book sales, council member office hours, or Neighborhood Action Committee meetings

The storytime boxes (see Chapter 5) were created before our kickoff date, and the community events were planned by people external to the library. This meant that the central unit had to plan the four central programs and the six programs in a box each month. (Actually, they had to plan many more than that so that each location could have different options from which to choose.) Central staff were also expected to coordinate the paid performers and possibly create box programs for the volunteers to lead, depending on the situation. In addition, they were required to create program descriptions for the menus so that the branches could choose which were appropriate for their community; write publicity blurbs for each program that would be used on the monthly calendars as well as in fliers; and create the monthly calendars for a subset of the branches.

The intent was that our full-time clerk would handle most of this, but once we saw how much time it took to create a program calendar, we quickly realized it would be impossible for her to handle the workload alone, and we divided this responsibility among the six of us . . . which, in turn, meant each librarian had less time for program planning and delivery. However, there were some days when five or more branches all wanted a program at the same time, and we sent the clerk out to present one. This could never have worked if my team of five were not the most collaborative, creative, hardworking people I could have imagined hiring!

The next year, when I'd moved on to another assignment, the central unit was moved to the main library's reference department. The idea was that the reference manager could supervise the team, and her existing clerical staff could provide more support than our single clerk could. This freed the librarians from the calendar assignments, but in turn, they were expected to work some hours on the reference desk.

Arapahoe (CO) Library District has a different model for centralized programming. Donna Geesaman is the youth program specialist, focusing on children from birth to age 11. The other four staff on their central team include a teen and adult specialist, a programming librarian, an administrative assistant, and a supervisor. At SJPL, I didn't really have specialists except informally (e.g., Leslie Tanaka was our go-to children's expert while Aleta Dimas covered a lot of the Spanish-language programming, but really, they were all generalists), but Arapahoe chose a different path. The central team at Arapahoe handles specialty programming and computer classes, but book clubs, storytimes, and many other recurring programs are planned and implemented locally (Cindy Mares, email message to author, February 21, 2013). Omaha Public Library also has an age-level model, with one librarian serving as an adult programming manager and another as the youth services coordinator, which includes children's, teen, and family programming (Amy Mather, email message to author, January 28, 2013).

Santa Cruz (CA) Public Library does it yet another way. Their 10-branch system has a central team of peers with no manager. A team leader is chosen by lottery each year from among the five librarians; each year's leader receives a temporary 5 percent pay increase as a stipend. The team also includes a clerical assistant for scheduling and for administrative tasks. All team members are full-time and report to an administrator. This group provides in-person programming for children and teens and creates box programs to be presented to youth by specially-trained volunteers; branch staff are all paraprofessionals and do not do any programming at all. The central team's heavy workload means that they focus only on youth programming, leaving the administrator to handle planning for adult classes and events (Janis O'Driscoll, in discussion with the author, February 25, 2013).

How will you determine how to staff your group? Like so many decisions related to changing your programming model, this too will depend on your library's structure, priorities, and project scope. If you're streamlining rather than centralizing, your central team might be very small, with perhaps just a single programming librarian to focus on the big picture, while the daily work is still done in individual departments. Or if you're centralizing only a piece, like paid performers, maybe you'll just need one clerical staff member to handle negotiation, contracts, and payments. There are as many ways to do this as there are libraries!

WRITING JOB DESCRIPTIONS

Once you've gotten past the craziness of figuring out how many staff you'll need and what they'll do, it's time to post job descriptions.

Sample job descriptions for central unit staff, based loosely on SJPL's job postings, are given below. Your descriptions will vary, depending on your model, but this will give you some idea of the duties and required skills.

Librarian

Primary Duties:

- Selects, develops, and coordinates programs based on input from branches/units
- Develops and coordinates box programs and resources for use by self, other programming librarians, or branch/unit staff
- Secures resources and coordinates planning for system-wide programs such as Summer Reading and One City/One Book

- Notifies the materials selectors of program plans to ensure that collections support upcoming programs
- Delivers planned programming to branches and units
- Identifies local partners for system-wide programs representing our diverse community
- Establishes and maintains ongoing relationships with partner agencies to address service response areas
- Explores partnership opportunities with other city departments
- Works with the volunteer coordinator to identify, recruit, and train self-directed volunteers to support programming
- Responds to library program inquiries from the media and public
- Distributes library information to schools at the district level
- Assigns daily work to the marketing support staff
- Liaises between branches and the programming unit
- Provides feedback on branch and community needs to programming unit as well as feedback on the programming model and how it can be improved
- May present language- or demographic-specific programs

Desirable Traits:

- Adaptable: thinks well on feet, responds positively to change
- Flexible: works well with all branches and communities, offers program variety, is willing to travel, can work a schedule that varies weekly
- Has a commitment to the centralized programming model and can be a cheerleader with staff and public
- Has strong interpersonal skills
- High energy, passionate
- Understands library and city priorities
- Can communicate at a high level, both in writing and orally
- Is able to promote and maintain effective public relations and outreach with a variety of communities and audiences
- Is highly skilled in customer service

Clerical Assistant

Primary Duties:

- Delivers programming menu for the system in collaboration with unit librarians
- Creates monthly programming calendars for branches
- Creates program fliers and slides
- Enters library events in the system and external event databases
- Maintains the program schedule for system units

- Processes contracts and payments for system programs, including W-9 forms for performers
- Tracks purchases and supply orders
- Represents the library via internal customer service to system units, suppliers, and contracted and potential programmers and performers

Desirable Traits:

- Excels at written and oral communication
- Demonstrates organizational and time-management skills
- Is able to prepare and maintain unit staffing budgets and timesheets
- Is familiar with Excel, Publisher, Word, PowerPoint, and SharePoint
- Can creatively offer services using technology
- Has understanding of and commitment to programming unit goals
- Has excellent customer service skills

INTERVIEWING CANDIDATES

For a change as radical as centralized programming, it makes the most sense to hire internally. After all, it's difficult enough to convince staff to accept that administration and your project team have enough local knowledge to make central programming work. Imagine how difficult it would be with outsiders coming in! Plus, those staff who have worked at branches and public service units in the past will be the most knowledgeable about local programming preferences, and their existing relationships with front-line staff mean that they will be agents of positive change in their own way.

For internal candidates, keep the interviews short. You already have some knowledge of who these people are, and instead of asking for references, you can talk to current and former supervisors and colleagues right there in your own organization. Some recommended questions to ask candidates for your clerical positions are:

Why are you the best candidate for this position?

To some, this question seems vague and unnecessary, but it is good to ask it in any interview. You will hear the candidate talk positively about himself, and be able to understand from his own word choices that he appreciates the necessary qualifications for and responsibilities of the role for which he's interviewing.

Tell me about your philosophy of internal customer service.

What you're looking for here is some acknowledgment that we have excellent internal relationships with colleagues system-wide, which is a critical part of this role.

How have you demonstrated the ability to be a team player?

In many library systems, it's difficult for a clerk to find opportunities to serve
on system-wide committees, cross-departmental teams, and so on. If a clerk
candidate has done this, that says a lot about her ability, but it is also helpful
to have the candidate talk about specific roles: did she lead the team, set up
the meetings, write the report, serve as a subject-matter specialist?

*Please describe your experience in a very busy environment with complex sched-
uling and few staff.*

Here, what you want to hear is some confirmation that the clerk is used to
working in a very busy branch or unit, or at another job before coming to
the library, and that he's accustomed to complicated schedules, last-minute
changes, and frequent demands on his time. Someone who can only do scheduling from home, for example, because he needs complete quiet for detailed
tasks, would not do well in the central programming unit.

For librarian candidates, asking the first two questions above is highly recommended, as well as the following:

*Please describe your experience planning and presenting programming for all
ages and for diverse cultures.*

The best answers here include a statement about being a generalist, at least, if
that's what you're looking for. If the candidate focuses on her experience with
just one age group or demographic group, ask her to talk about her experiences
with different kinds of customers. Or ask her to differentiate between a program
she'd do on a certain topic for teenagers versus one targeted at senior citizens.

*The programming unit will have several librarians working together as a team.
How would you collaborate with your colleagues, and what would be your
contributions?*

After you've established an ability to work as a generalist with the question
above, you're now looking for the librarian's actual interests and talents . . .
not just relating to programming ability, but to group work in general. Good
answers here would include that the librarian is flexible, works well as either
a leader or a foot soldier, can both plan and present programming, has connections to the relevant community agencies, can speak certain languages, and
so on. The collaboration part of the question should result in an answer that
indicates the candidate is able to both teach and learn from the other team
members.

*Are you able to work a flexible schedule that will change every week and will
include evenings, weekends, and plenty of local travel?*

This is a good place to find out whether the librarian has a reliable car, if he
has childcare responsibilities on certain days that can't be changed, or if he is
nervous going to certain parts of town. Some scheduling unavailability can be
worked around, but in general, you need librarians who can present programming during any of the library's open hours, and perhaps at outreach events,
when the library may be closed.

HIRING THE RIGHT PEOPLE

Choosing the right candidates has a lot more to do with you and your organization than it does with criteria laid out in a book by a stranger, so take this advice with a grain of salt: You'll want to choose a team with complementary skills, so you don't want three teen specialists in your central unit. You'll want to pick people who have a reputation for getting along well with others so you don't have to spend your time solving infighting. You want positive, flexible people with strong work ethics. Overall, you want people who have answered your questions and responded positively to the idea of centralization, and who have the potential to contribute to a team that is more than the sum of its parts.

WORKSPACES

Your new staff need a large workspace with lots of storage for boxes, books, supplies, and more. They will work even more collaboratively than most library staff, and therefore, need a common space where they can see and hear one another—which also means a space where others will not be bothered by their noise. The clerical staff also need private space where they can work quietly and focus on details. Realistically, your staff's workspace will be wherever there is room in your building, but try to include as much of the above as you can.

Staffing is perhaps the most critical element of centralized programming. Be sure to select your staff with great care and to give them the resources they need to succeed. In addition to doing the everyday work of the unit, they're your ambassadors to the other staff, so do what you can to ensure their morale and productivity.

5

Program Development: Storytime

Storytime is such a central and essential component of public library programming that it deserves its own chapter in this book—and requires special treatment when considering centralizing or streamlining programming as well. As part of a completely centralized programming implementation, storytime must still be considered separately. In fact, if you're not completely centralizing yet, but want to pilot a piece of the model, storytime is a great piece to do first.

WHAT IS STORYTIME IN A BOX?

Simply put, a Storytime in a Box is a collection of materials that any librarian should be able to use to put on a week's worth of themed storytimes. Librarians should be able to familiarize themselves with the box's contents in 30 minutes or less (or whatever benchmark you set), and should be able to adapt the box's contents to work with a variety of age groups. The box should contain all the physical ingredients of a successful storytime, whatever that means at your library: books for babies, toddlers, preschoolers, and school-aged children; a CD or playlist of songs, with laminated lyrics sheets; fingerplay instructions and videos; coloring sheets; puppets; manipulatives; nametags; stickers; and/or whatever other components add up to a great storytime experience at your library. Each piece of paper in the box should be laminated, if possible, since many people will handle it over the year.

WHAT STORYTIME IN A BOX IS *NOT*

There are some things that Storytime in a Box is not:

- It is not a pre-packaged box that you buy complete. Such packages are available, and some of them are of good quality, but it is not recommended that you purchase them for this project. Using materials your library already owns results in cost savings, and having librarians customize the contents of your boxes creates a giant step toward staff buy-in.

- It is not a substitute for a trained storyteller. Certainly, someone with initiative but no experience can pick up a box and figure out how to use it, but this will take longer than your 30-minute benchmark.

- It is not a box that can be used for every single storytime some branches might offer. For example, your library may offer storytimes in the Russian language, but only at two of your 20 branches. It wouldn't make sense to include Russian books and songs in your storytime boxes since they would be so infrequently used, and besides, this would remove them unnecessarily from the circulating collection.

STORYTIME IN A BOX TASK FORCE

Storytime is so beloved by librarians, as well as the public, that it can be especially difficult to get buy-in from your librarians to centralize this function, particularly the ones who are already well-known for delivering excellent storytimes to your community's families. Think about who that might be in your library. You can probably come up with a few names on your own, or ask your youth services manager. From these names, you will be able to form a small team, perhaps one person for every three to five branches, to serve as your Storytime in a Box Task Force.

Whom do you want to serve on this team? Of course, you want those who are known for creating excellent storytimes. However, it's also important to think back to Chapter 2 and select the right mix of Red, Yellow, and Green librarians for your task force. You'll want a Green librarian as the team leader; this should be someone who's perceived as an authority figure, but is also good at collaboration. Perhaps this could be the youth services manager or a respected storytime veteran at your library system. If neither of these are Green librarians, an administrator or someone else from your program team or another manager who is Green could stand in to lead the group. Remember, the team leader plays a critical and sensitive role. She will have to organize a team of librarians, with differing degrees of reluctance, and lead them to create resources that can be used throughout your library system by librarians whose experience varies dramatically. She will have to ensure the quality of the boxes as well as the goodwill of her team, since the team will be training others on how to use the boxes.

PLANNING THE BOXES

Now that you have your task force, it's time to determine the parameters for your particular library system. The questions you'll want the team to consider include the following:

1. *What goes into a high-quality storytime and how can the boxes reflect that?*
   Besides efficiency, one of the best reasons to centralize storytime programming is to ensure a more consistent experience across all locations in your
   library system. Families often travel to various branches to find the schedule
   that works best for them, and they might find huge differences in quality.
   At one branch, a longtime storyteller might provide a full-fledged eight-part
   storytime with songs, fingerplays, a puppet show, dancing, and flannelboards
   in addition to stories. At another, a newer librarian may decide to focus on
   the books and forget what she considers to be fluff. At a third, someone with
   no training might create a fun music and story hour, strumming his guitar
   and reading a themed book at the end. All of these may be wonderful for the
   children who attend, but each has its problems as well as its delights. Your
   team should determine the components of a successful storytime and be sure
   to include materials in the boxes to support their vision.

2. *What is our budget for this project and how can we spend it for maximum
   impact?*
   This will vary dramatically by library, and specific budgeting is beyond the
   scope of this book. However, you will need to budget for the following:

   - X number of books per box, if not coming from your circulating collection
     (see below)
   - Puppets, flannelboard pieces, etc.
   - Blank CDs
   - Stickers, nametags, or other handouts
   - A laminating machine
   - A color printer
   - Sturdy boxes for routing. These are pricy but worth it.
   - Basic supplies and equipment you expect each branch to have, such as scis-
     sors, paper, crayons, whiteboard, and CD player, so that you don't have to
     route the basics each time

3. *Where will we get the components?*
   It's best to use books that are in your existing collection. Your picture book
   selectors put great care into choosing books that children and families love,
   maintaining a strong supply of the classics and award-winners as well as
   keeping abreast of new books that have had positive reviews among children
   and librarians alike. They might initially object to seeing those titles move off
   the shelves and into boxes, but you can remind them that if a given book is
   used at every branch at least once a week, it's reaching more readers than if
   it's checked out by one family at a time during the same period.

   If you maintain two separate collections, as many libraries do—one of circulating copies, one of noncirculating copies just for storytime—you run the
   risk of these two collections not matching. It's easy for your storytime collection to grow stale when you aren't adding to it on a regular basis, as you
   are with your circulating collection. This often doesn't stop librarians from
   wanting to keep a storytime collection anyway, though that includes titles

that aren't in your circulating collection. A librarian might say, "But this is a classic. Children have loved this book for fifty years. We don't have a copy on the shelf, so I need to keep this one for storytime." But if the book is so beloved, why have your selectors not chosen it for the circulating collection? If it's out of print, again, how did it go out of print if it's so popular? The moral here is to trust the specialized expertise of your staff. Trust your selectors to select, and your storytime task force to choose from among those books for programming purposes.

Of course, there are also budget implications for using books from your existing collection. You won't have the initial cost of making a big book purchase just for the boxes. You will, however, want to make sure that there are multiple copies of your storytime box books still circulating, so that parents can check out the same books they've heard your librarians read aloud.

Bringing all the available copies to storytime will make life a little easier for parents at checkout time, and will also have the advantage of boosting circulation. In addition, it can be a cue for your librarians to see which books the families liked most; if you read four books and bring several copies of each to storytime, and you end up re-shelving only one title, that's the one that held the least fascination for your customers that day.

There is one important exception to the "use your own circulating collection" rule: pop-up books that are easily damaged while they are checked out. It's really best to purchase your own copies of books with pop-ups, lift-the-flap pages, or other delicate elements, so that they're in great shape during storytime. But these should still be additional copies of titles that are already in the circulating collection.

How do you make sure you have the books you need in your boxes, and still account for them in your catalog? At San José Public Library (SJPL), I asked our circulation manager to create a new customer type in our library software that would allow these books to be checked out for an entire calendar year. We considered merely suppressing these items from public view or changing the status to "library staff use," but decided against these ideas. Suppressing particular copies would have made it more difficult to switch copies in and out of boxes if we misplaced one or found one in better condition. Changing the status would send the wrong message to customers browsing the catalog—that staff needs were more important than customers' needs—and would also imply that perhaps customers could check out those copies if they talked to staff about it. Checking out the books with an extended due date, and receiving email notifications when they were due, would remind the centralized programming staff that they needed to renew or replace the titles in question when the year was up. Of course, some customers did ask why, in October 2010, they were looking in the catalog at an item due date of July 2011, but these were few and far between, and staff were easily able to explain.

4. *How many boxes do we need?*
The logistics of box delivery can be a real source of angst for librarians who have no control over delivery drivers' schedules or priorities. Their hearts are

in the right place, of course; they want to offer high-quality programming without having to worry over a truck's flat tire or a driver who called in sick. Because of this, when I developed the storytime box logistics for SJPL, it was a priority to ensure that every branch had a backup box as well as the box they planned to use that week. We had 19 locations (18 branches and a main library with a very busy children's room), so we planned on a total of 38 boxes plus two spares, and built 40 boxes.

BUILDING THE BOXES

Creating storytime boxes can be a fun team-building activity if you plan it right. In San José, I reserved one of our most appealing meeting rooms with large windows, internet access, and plenty of space to spread out for this endeavor. The Storytime Box Task Force used this room all day on four separate days spread across a three-week period.

What did they do for four days? So much! They started out by developing 40 themes, one for each box we planned. Themes included Monkeys, Back to School, Healthy Eating, and many more. Then, they divided up the boxes among themselves based on their individual preferences and expertise.

Each librarian took his set of assigned box themes and jotted down ideas for titles. They emailed the system's children's librarians to ask for anything they might have missed ("I'm building the Cats and Kittens box. What would you recommend for storytime besides *Mr. Pusskins: A Love Story* and *Kitten's First Full Moon?*"), and verified the title availability in our catalog. A guideline was that no book should be included in a box unless we had at least five circulating copies in the system. If they really wanted to include a book but didn't have ample copies, they asked the children's selector to consider ordering more.

The librarians placed holds on these books and then began searching for supplemental materials. Each branch had a veritable storehouse of puppets, stuffed animals, flannelboard pieces, CDs, stickers, and other storytime props that were generally used only once a year. We had earlier asked for any of these items that had been purchased by the library (as opposed to the personal items of individual librarians, which were also in heavy use) to be shipped to the main library for sorting and evaluation. We ended up tossing much of this material, such as ratty puppets or faded flannel pieces, but there was also a lot of quality material left at the end. We had clerical staff sort these into the 40 themes so that the task force members could select what they wanted and discard or donate the rest.

After the task force was finished finding new homes for the materials we owned, it was time to create and/or purchase things to fill in the gaps. Each task-force librarian looked at her boxes and thought about what else was needed to provide a comprehensive storytime. We had decided that the ideal box contained at least one puppet, flannelboard, or other manipulative, so we ordered high-quality versions of those to supplement what we had.

In the meantime, the books on which we'd placed holds were coming in from all around the system. When we placed these holds, we'd intentionally done it at the item level so we could ensure we weren't depleting the picture book collections of just a handful of branches. We also wanted to make sure not to take the last copy of any title from any location. As the books came in, we checked their condition, and requested a different copy in the cases where the one we had was looking dilapidated. Sometimes, this meant emailing the children's librarian at a branch and asking him to choose the prettiest copy from the five on shelf. When we had the right books in the right condition, clerical staff checked them out to the Storytime Box library card we'd created, and sorted them into the right boxes.

LANGUAGE BOXES

Many library systems provide regular storytimes in languages other than English. In most cases, this will vary from branch to branch, with Spanish being critical in some locations but Korean in others, while others don't have a need for storytimes except in English. Because of this variation, it's probably best not to include language materials in your English storytime boxes. Picture book collections in other languages may be sparse, and you won't want to remove those materials from your circulating collection only to have them sit in boxes where they are rarely used.

A better idea, if you have a group of branches all using a specific language, is to create a smaller set of boxes in that language and feature a separate rotation among just that group of branches. For example, if just one of your 12 branches does a storytime in Japanese—the librarians at the branch in question can use puppets and flannelboards from your English-language box, but supplement them with Japanese books and CDs from the selection available at the branch.

HOLIDAY BOXES

When developing the themes for the storytime boxes, a question that always seems to come up is what to do about the holidays. Yes, you could pick Halloween as one of your box themes, but since the boxes are in rotation, what about the branch that gets the Halloween box in April? One solution is to create virtual boxes for each holiday your library system celebrates at storytime. Rather than pulling books from shelves and routing them among your branches, create a list online of Halloween books librarians could choose for each age level throughout Halloween week. Your task force should choose these titles with the same care they used to put holds on physical books, ensuring the titles are owned by each branch or are easy to acquire from a neighboring location. Lists can also include suggested songs available on circulating CDs or available for free online, and perhaps craft projects, if your library includes those in storytimes. The lists can live on your intranet or wherever you store other documentation related to programming, such as programs in virtual boxes (see Chapter 6). Then, your storytellers can incorporate elements from that week's storytime boxes to create a complete Halloween storytime.

ROTATION AND DELIVERY

The rotation and delivery of the boxes is the topic I'm asked about most when I speak about centralized programming at conferences or networking events. The best-planned storytimes done by the most beloved of storytellers can be derailed if the box of materials doesn't get to its destination on time. Pay close attention to the logistical aspects of your storytime box rotation to ensure this doesn't happen to you.

The boxes themselves are the first element of a strong logistical plan. Choose sturdy boxes that close tightly and can stand up to being on the bottom of six bins of books in a delivery truck. In San José, we chose to purchase the same boxes that we already used to transport materials between branches; these were expensive but worth it, as they would easily stack, the drivers were used to handling them, and we knew they could tolerate the stresses of the delivery process. We had hoped to get the same boxes in a different color to easily differentiate from the book bins, but this wasn't possible; we settled for the same gray bins but decorated the sides so that branch and delivery staff could distinguish them from the book bins.

The bins in which books, movies, and music were transferred between branches didn't have lids, but we did purchase lids for the storytime boxes. Each box was labeled on top with the complete list of locations to rotate it among. When the first branch was done with a box, they'd cross out their location, and the delivery staff would pick it up and deliver it to the next branch on the list.

As mentioned earlier, my team created 40 boxes: two for each branch to start with, plus two extras, just in case. Librarians were concerned that if there were any problems with delivery, they'd be left boxless for the coming week, so we made sure they each started out with two boxes but routed just one away at the end of each week. This way, they always had a backup box.

For example, Branch A began with the Dinosaurs box and the Dogs & Puppies box. They chose to use Dinosaurs as the week's storytime theme, and on the Saturday of that week, they put their Dinosaurs box out for delivery to the next branch. On Monday, they received the Sun, Moon, & Stars box from another branch, and they got to choose whether to do Sun, Moon, & Stars storytimes or Dogs & Puppies storytimes that week. They chose Dogs & Puppies, and so routed that one away on Saturday of the second week, and so on throughout the year.

We made 40 storytime boxes, even though we only needed 38, just because 40 was a round number. It turned out that this was a good call—we needed those two extras! In one case, a branch librarian known for his high-quality storytimes was asked by the local councilmember to do an abbreviated storytime at a City Council meeting. We gladly shipped the librarian one of our extra boxes so he could have plenty of time to prepare. In the other case, one of our boxes already in rotation was getting very poor reviews by library staff. The theme was Five Senses, and in retrospect, we saw that this was too broad to make a good storytime. We pulled the Five Senses box and replaced it with our other spare.

The beauty of the rotating storytime box model is that it can be adapted to fit libraries of any size. If your large county library system has 55 branches, you can scale up to make more boxes. If, however, you're in a single-building library, you can scale back. In this case, you don't need to rotate among locations, but you might plan a year's worth of weekly themes and make purchases ahead of time, then build boxes *after* each storytime for reuse next year. You probably wouldn't include circulating items in this case, to avoid taking them off the shelf for a full year. Or, of course, you can change your rotation cycle to be every six months or every three years instead of each year. There are infinite variations on the storytime box plan; you can develop one to suit your needs.

REDUCING LOCAL PREP TIME

Since one of the key reasons for implementing storytime boxes is to save planning time, it's a good idea to provide librarians and managers with guidelines on how much time to spend with each box. For example, you could say that librarians should spend no more than 30 minutes with the storytime box when it comes in each week, and then, no more than 15 minutes prepping for each individual storytime (15 minutes before the Tuesday Toddler Time, 15 minutes before Wednesday's lapsit program, and 15 minutes before family storytime on Saturday morning). This can be adjusted in the case of a language storytime, where books need to be chosen from outside the box, or for the holiday storytimes, where the box is only virtual and books can be chosen from an online list. Individual managers may also want to adapt the timeline to allow a brand-new storyteller some additional preparation time.

Because storytime is so beloved, and many librarians have spent years honing their skills in preparation as well as performance, this can be a difficult struggle. Some of your Red librarians will try to ignore the boxes altogether and continue to develop their storytimes from scratch. This is when it's important to have the buy-in of their managers, who can help to remind the librarians of the important reasons for doing this, and can schedule their time to ensure they are no longer putting in as much prep time. One way to help manage this from a system level is to ask managers to schedule specific amounts of prep time for each storytime. The effectiveness of this will depend on how much oversight administration has over scheduling; at SJPL, we had a centralized scheduling software program, so this was easier than it might be in a system where scheduling is done on paper or where librarians' time is not scheduled on an hourly basis.

It's helpful to create very clear guidelines about how to use the boxes, and to share these guidelines with managers first to get their input and buy-in. Then, managers will be empowered to work individually with librarians who may have difficulty accepting the new routine. It can be helpful to let these managers and librarians know that it's perfectly fine to include many of their traditional, personalized storytime elements! For example, while you don't want librarians researching new songs or searching for new books from the shelves, they are welcome to sing songs they already know, such as their standard opening and closing songs, or other favorites. They can continue to delight children with musical instruments they have always played at storytime. A favorite stuffed animal who always greeted the children at the beginning of storytime can still do so! The point of storytime boxes isn't to create identical, cookie-cutter programming system-wide; it's to cut down dramatically on prep time by doing most of the work upfront.

INVENTORYING AND LOSS

Each of your storytime boxes should contain a laminated inventory sheet that branch librarians can go over when they first open the box. As the librarian looks at each piece, she can check the sheet to find out if anything is missing, and call the branch that last had the box so that they can look around for it. At the bottom of the inventory sheet, you could list the virtual components of your box, such as a YouTube video demonstrating how to do a fingerplay, so that librarians remember these resources are available too.

Sometimes, a puppet or a CD will go missing and no one will be able to find it. Make sure to assign a central contact, such as a programming clerk, the responsibility for re-purchasing and replacing lost items, such as a lost teddy bear or re-burning a missing CD—and make sure that all the branch librarians know whom to contact in this case. If you frequently find that pieces are missing and no one can find them, you might consider having your boxes route through your central programming or youth services department once or twice during their regular rotation, where central staff can take responsibility for inventory and replacement pieces.

Another issue relating to box inventory and loss is storytime hiatuses. Designating two or three times per year when your library system doesn't offer storytime is a good idea because it gives your storytellers a much-needed break to avoid burnout. It can also serve as the time period when all boxes are routed back to the central office for inventory and restocking. Of course, remember to ensure that your hiatuses happen during the lowest-attendance times of the year for storytime, such as the winter holidays or the first month of school.

ALTERNATIVES TO STORYTIME BOXES

There are many ways to centralize storytime. Storytime can still be centralized, even if you don't want to use boxes. At Santa Cruz (CA) Public Library, the centralized programming team delivers storytimes in person. Their branches are close enough to one another that this is feasible from a time-management perspective. At first, central storytellers divided the storytimes among themselves by age level, so that one would perform all the baby storytimes and one the preschool storytimes, and so on. They soon realized that branches preferred to see the same familiar faces each week, and they were easily able to adapt to this by dividing the 10 branches among the five librarians. Now, each librarian has a closer relationship with two particular branches, which not only satisfies the parents, but also makes that librarian better able to predict what other types of programming would best suit the branch. These five librarians are still able to maximize efficiency by sitting down together and creating themes a few months ahead of time, which enables them to work together on book lists, share costs, and ensure consistent program delivery, no matter which branch a customer attends.

At Arapahoe (CO) Public Library, storytimes are presented by central staff, but rather than their programming team, it's handled by the Child and Family Library Services department. At Baltimore County Public Library, a team of centralized staff, supplemented by volunteers, delivers storytimes to each location.

These strategies may work well for your library if, as in some of the above-mentioned systems, your branch staff is primarily composed of paraprofessionals or reference librarians who have little experience in delivering storytime. Each of these solutions is a step in the right direction: efficiency, quality, and consistency.

6

Program Development: Other Staffed Programs

In this chapter, you'll learn about staffed programs—programs in a box, programs in a virtual box, and programs presented by your central programming unit.

DEFINITIONS

Let's start with some definitions:

- A *program in a box* is a program developed by your central team, with physical components packed in a box, with instructions included, and delivered to a branch or unit to be presented by local staff. Storytime boxes and craft programs are common box programs.

- A *program in a virtual box* is similar, except that there is no physical component (such as craft supplies) necessary, and so the box can be delivered online via intranet, email, or the cloud. Computer classes are popular virtual-box programs.

- A *centrally-delivered program* is one that is developed by your central team and also presented by them. They plan the program, pack up any necessary supplies, and drive out to the location offering the program to present it in person.

PROGRAMS IN A BOX

Storytime is the quintessential program in a box—it is thoroughly covered in Chapter 5. Craft programs and gaming sessions are also excellent candidates for box programs.

Since consistent quality combined with efficiency are the goals of program streamlining, it's important that you decide upfront what supplies branches and units will be expected to provide themselves, and which ones you will pack into a box. For example, at San José Public Library (SJPL), every branch was expected to have a flannelboard, meaning that we could put flannel pieces into every box and not worry about routing the boards. Similarly, for craft projects, ask the branches and units to purchase (or you could purchase for them and deliver) a set of basic supplies, such as construction paper, glue, crayons, and a stapler. Additional supplies, ranging from glitter to stickers to yarn to doilies to beads to clay, should be included in the boxes for each craft that requires them. This means you must be careful not to leave off your basic supply list something that most crafts need, such as scissors.

When you build box programs, it's ideal to include not only supplies and instructions, but a finished version of the craft to be used as a model for both staff and customers. Even better are pictures of what the craft should look like at each step of the way. The librarian or other staff member designated to present the program to customers may not be as craft-savvy as your central team member who created it. You may even want to create two versions of your craft using most of the same supplies—a more difficult version for crafty librarians and an easier one for novices. This could also turn into one version for teens and one for children, or one for adults and one for teens. That way, it becomes two programs in one box!

Either when you're beginning centralized programming or as you go forward, ask the branch staff to create box programs based on their successful past events. That way, you can cultivate local talent in a manner that allows all branches to benefit.

Here are just a few examples of box programs:

Teen Movie in a Box

Of course, this box will contain a DVD of the movie to show. It could also have snacks, trivia questions (especially book vs. movie questions, if applicable), and any promotional giveaways related to the movie. Brooke Ballard, teen librarian at San Antonio Public Library, puts popcorn and Kool-Aid in her teen movie boxes. You could also include bags of chips, and pretzels, boxes of movie theater candy, bottled water, or whatever works best for teens at your library. You might consider asking a local grocery store to contribute snacks in exchange for acknowledgement of their sponsorship on your publicity materials.

Book Club in a Box

Many book clubs prefer to select their own books, which is terrific—but some don't. For new book clubs just starting out, or perhaps a children's after-school club, this box could include 10 to 20 copies of the book, a list of discussion questions (both generic and book-specific), and perhaps tie-ins, such as bookmarks or a snack related to the book. The materials should be detailed enough that a staff member or volunteer who hasn't read the book can still facilitate the discussion. You could also consider a "genre book club" box, where you include a variety of titles in a single genre, such as mystery or fantasy, and then create discussion questions that apply to that genre, as well as some that are book-specific. This means your discussion will have a less in-depth focus on a specific title; however, it means exposing your group to a broader range of books that are still within a genre they enjoy.

Knitting Nook in a Box

This is a great program for a volunteer to lead, or a staff member (like a shelver) who doesn't usually do programming but loves to knit. Knitting has become very popular, so chances are you'll be able to easily recruit someone to lead this group. But even if the branch or unit doesn't have a knitter, you can still offer Knitting Nook in a Box. If a staff member is willing to learn to knit from YouTube videos, customers new to knitting can learn alongside her. Your program can be as simple or complex as you like; your audience may prefer a casual evening of knitting and chatting, or maybe they'd like to include some formal instruction on beginners' or advanced knitting techniques. Perhaps they would all like to contribute to a single finished product, or maybe they want advice on knitting special holiday gifts.

Dr. Seuss's Birthday in a Box

Lots of branches will want this in early March to celebrate the author's birthday. You can include supplies for goofy hats, instructions for writing Seussian poems, blank books for writing your own Sam (or insert your name)-I-Am books . . . the possibilities are endless. Include a few Dr. Seuss books, of course, or a suggested book list so librarians can supplement their storytime boxes that week. Since many parents and children will know only Seuss's best-known titles like *The Cat in the Hat* and *Green Eggs and Ham*, be sure to include those, but you could also expand their horizons with titles not quite as well-known, such as *If I Ran the Zoo* and *A Great Day for Up*. A lower-key approach might be to create a Dr. Seuss storytime to add to your list of virtual holiday storytimes (see Chapter 5).

Teen Book-Buying Party in a Box

This was the invention of teen librarians Kat Luedke and Birgit Vogler at SJPL. They worked together on a project to involve teen volunteer clubs in the choice of materials for their age group, so they brought some laptops to Kat's next teen meeting and tried to interest the teens in online selection. Surprisingly, the teens much preferred to work with paper catalogs, so Birgit and Kat enlisted library staff attending conferences to hit the exhibit halls and pick up as many as they could. They offered music, snacks, and advice ("Think about what other teens like to read, not just what you like") and it was a hit. Later, when Birgit joined my central team, she and Kat easily turned this into a program in a box that every branch could host.

PROGRAMS IN A VIRTUAL BOX

These are easy to create for any program that doesn't include a physical component. Computer classes are a good place to begin; if every branch is offering an Introduction to Microsoft Excel class or Facebook for Seniors, there's no need for everyone to reinvent the wheel. Ask branches to submit their class materials to you, pick the best set (or combine several, if you prefer), and upload them to your intranet for remote sites to download. If you don't have an intranet, you can use a free wiki site, a service like Dropbox or Google Drive, or even just email.

Computer Class in a Box

There are hundreds of topics you can cover in a computer class, from Introduction to Computers to Pinterest for Small Businesses. The best virtual boxes will include a script for the teacher, handouts for the students, and a tip sheet ("Many students fumble with achieving X; seniors often have difficulty with Y, but it's easier if you ask them to Z first"). If you're doing a demo rather than a hands-on class, you will want to include a PowerPoint as well.

Mock Citizenship Interview in a Box

Most large cities today have many residents who are working toward citizenship. You can create a variety of programs to help them toward this goal; one of the most popular is the mock citizenship interview. Your box program can include a list of the questions that may be asked (available at www.uscis.gov), as well as a script for teaching the material covered and a list of other resources and related agencies.

CENTRALLY PRESENTED PROGRAMS

Some programs simply don't work as routed boxes or virtual downloads. For example, we found that the Bubble Science program SJPL offered in our very first month of centralized programming was better delivered centrally. This was because we couldn't have routed gallons of dish soap, big tubs for water, piles of aprons, or giant bubble wands very easily. Plus, this program was a messy, outdoors type of activity; which was tons of fun, but might have been a difficult sell to some branches. So we sent out our intrepid central team to do it instead.

Even for simpler activities such as a science experiment or an introduction to social media, it might be best to offer the program first as a centrally-presented program. Then, your team can finetune a craft, for example, before writing up instructions and sending it out for all to try. Seeing where a student got stuck or realizing you forgot to include a hole punch is helpful to know in advance so you can pack the right supplies and help branch presenters avoid pitfalls.

CENTRAL RECIPES

Omaha Public Library splits the difference between locally- and centrally-presented programs by creating central "recipes" for programs, including lists of supplies that are the branches' responsibilities to obtain. For example, their "Board Silly" program—an adult board game party—includes a variety of suggested games as well as instructions for acquiring a liquor license, checking IDs, and so on. Another program recipe is for a workshop where customers can make their own eco-friendly toiletries and household cleaners; this includes a shopping list, instructions, and even a short list of leftovers from other branches' iterations of this workshop.

Whatever mix of box, virtual box, and centrally-staffed programs your library chooses to provide, it's important to remember that your team doesn't have to create them all. You'll reduce the chance of burnout for your central team while also promoting local creativity if you harness branch talent to help you develop this set of options. This also applies to the next chapter on external presenters, as branch staff will be able to tell you which performers are worthwhile and which aren't a good fit for their branch or the system.

7

Program Development: Partner, Volunteer, and Paid Programs

Not all programs are presented by library staff. After all, your staff can't be expected to have expertise in every area; some topics are too complex or specific. Luckily, others in your community have knowledge they may be willing to share—partners, volunteers, and paid presenters.

DEFINITIONS

In this book, the types of program providers are differentiated as follows:

- A *programming partner* is an agency, group, or company that has expertise in a particular topic and will provide a program on that topic, either free of charge or for in-kind compensation.
- A *volunteer* is similar to a partner, except that volunteers are individuals (or families) with special knowledge or abilities, not groups or organizations. Volunteers are unpaid.
- A *paid presenter* is just that—a person or group that you pay to provide a program at your library.

PARTNER PROGRAMS

Santa Cruz Public Libraries (SCPL) said it best—"Partnerships and collaborations are essential to our service model. We have found these to be a successful way of providing services, strengthening bonds with the community, and keeping our programming fresh" (Bowen et al., 2011, 30). All three of these factors combine to make partner programs a terrific way to streamline programming, and they are easy to fit into a streamlined or centralized programming plan.

PROVIDING SERVICES

Partner agencies exist to provide services to the community, just as your library does. Their specific expertise can fill gaps in your staff's knowledge as well as provide extra pizzazz. Sure, your children's librarian could learn about fire safety and teach it to his storytime group, but if the local fire department comes in with uniforms and a big red truck, it's more fun and the message will last longer—and your librarian won't have to do much in the way of prep, especially with centralization.

STRENGTHENING BONDS WITH THE COMMUNITY

No public library in the country has yet convinced 100 percent of the residents in its service area to sign up for library cards. And not all of your cardholders use the library regularly or know about the full range of services you provide. So, one benefit of partnering with other agencies is finding new users. If you ask the parks and recreation department to come in to do a talk about bicycle safety, and if they promote it at their own facilities, then you might gain some first-time visitors to the library in addition to educating your existing users about helmets and u-locks.

Plus, the same pool of tax dollars that supports your library also funds other local, state, and federal government agencies. Intergovernmental cooperation means taxpayers get more bang for their bucks. For example, if you bring in a state park ranger to do a program on birding or a high school cross-country coach to talk about marathon prep, you avoid having to pay someone (including your own staff) for those purposes. Of course, tax dollars are also saved via nongovernmental partnerships; if you're not spending the money on a paid chess teacher but going through a local chess club instead, that's still a worthwhile endeavor.

At many public libraries, only Friends groups are authorized to sell books and other materials inside the library's facilities. At SCPL, the central team capitalized on this to authorize the Friends to plan and organize author programs. That way, authors could sell books within the library, offering them an additional incentive to do the program in the first place, and the Friends could contribute to the promotion of reading in a nontraditional way.

KEEPING PROGRAMMING FRESH

Have you had the same set of programs for years? Storytime, basic computing, Summer Reading, tax help, arts and crafts? Partners can really refresh your program calendar. Even the most eclectic, passionate, and talented staff have limits on what they can offer. Have you ever had a program on beachcombing? Ask a lifeguard or other knowledgeable person to come in (unless you're landlocked!). Which nonfiction books circulate the most?

Sewing, public speaking, making your own will? Consider bringing in local experts and authors to cover these topics. Many clubs, whether organized such as Toastmasters or just a group of friends who get together to quilt, would be happy to send representatives to talk about their hobbies at no cost, just for the pleasure of talking to others about their interest. Be careful, though; just because someone is a model-train enthusiast doesn't mean they're a good speaker or teacher. You'll want to meet these people in person or talk to others who have seen them speak to make sure your program will be interesting and useful.

Timeliness is also a factor. Given enough time, the right librarian can learn all there is to know about a local issue and then present on the topic. However, this isn't practical if you want to remain nimble and be able to respond to community issues as they occur. In Arlington Heights, Illinois, a sudden infestation of emerald ash borer, an insect that kills ash trees, had left village homeowners frustrated and worried. The public library partnered with the village's arborist as well as a state tree specialist to get information to the residents as quickly as possible through a series of programs.

DEVELOPING PARTNERSHIPS

There is an art and a science to partnership development, and a complete discussion of it is beyond the scope of this book. However, generally, when seeking programming partners, look at what your community needs. Fire safety for preschoolers? SAT prep classes? Information about the Affordable Care Act? Then, consider your community's local agencies and think about which might have expertise in the program topics you'd like to cover.

However, it's critical to remember that partnerships are two-way relationships. It's not just about you calling up another agency to see what they can offer your customers. Think about what you can give them in turn, or what you are already giving them. Visit potential partners' websites and read their mission statements. Are they in alignment with your library's vision and values? If so, how can you help? Can you distribute YMCA program schedules at branches near Y facilities? Does your information desk refer customers to a particular legal-aid society or adult literacy center? Would any of your branches be interested in handing out bookmarks at storytime advertising a Head Start program? Think about your library's role in the community and what matches your goals as well as your potential partner's. For more information on developing partnerships, see *Partnering with Purpose* (Crowther and Trott, 2004) and *Children's Services* (Diamant-Cohen, ed., 2010).

PARTNERSHIP PITFALLS

Working with community partners is a rewarding experience and great customer service, and it can also be quite efficient. One of the advantages to the centralization of programs is that it can eliminate the redundancy of 20 branches each calling the county dentists' association to schedule a Tooth Time storytime. Rather than all of that duplicate work, your central team can make one phone call, find out available days and times for the dentists to visit, and then offer them via your programming menu.

However, not all agencies are centralized in this way, which can be a headache for your staff. In some cases, there is no headquarters for your staff to contact; each local group is self-governing and accustomed to working with just the one or two library branches nearest them. Or sometimes, a particular organization covers only specific zip codes or serves only speakers of a certain language, so if you partner with them, you can only offer their programs to a subset of your branches. None of this has to be deal-breaking for your potential partnerships, but be aware that just because you've centralized doesn't mean that other groups have also done so.

After you've spent some time working with a variety of programming partners, you'll get to know the pros and cons of each organization—who's reliable, who can match your timelines (some groups aren't able to plan as far in advance as you may need to do), and so on. It takes time and trust to build a really successful partnership, and your second and third years of centralization may go more smoothly in this area than the first year.

It can also be frustrating for both you and your partners when you build a relationship and then offer their programs on your menu, but no or very few branches select that program. At San José Public Library (SJPL), this resulted in some menu modifications during the second year. The central team knew by that point that if they offered branches three partner programs per month from a list of six, the three selected were likely to be those predicted to get the biggest audiences. However, since children's programs tend to draw the biggest crowds, this meant that everyone was choosing those, and no one would select, say, a presenter on strategies for low-income home repairs. So the central team began to offer the home-repair program as a bonus in addition to the three branch choices. This helped both the partner organization and the target audience.

VOLUNTEER PROGRAMS

Many, if not most, libraries offer volunteer opportunities. Generally, these include sorting and shelving materials, greeting customers, pulling holds, or delivering materials to homebound customers. Rarely do libraries rely on the specialized skills of community members to provide targeted programming, although it's easy and low-cost to do so. A few examples of volunteer-led programs might be as follows:

- Someone with an expertise in knitting, crocheting, quilting, and so on could lead a weekly club or class

- A current or retired professional could offer programming in her area of expertise—résumé review by a human resources manager, writers' club by an English teacher, an overview of careers in journalism by a reporter
- The customer who always asks you for more book clubs or more programming on a certain topic could be asked to run one himself

Working with volunteers can be extremely rewarding for your staff, your volunteers, and your customers. Someone willing to come and work at the library for free can warm the hearts of even your Red staff members. The volunteers themselves will be advocates for your library in general as well as for library volunteerism. And, of course, your customers can't lose with local expertise offered free of charge.

Much like library staff, volunteers can take on more complex programming if they are trained appropriately. In 2002, Baltimore County Public Library formed a group of volunteers called Story Timers. These high-impact volunteers are selected and trained by the system's early literacy coordinator and deliver storytimes throughout the county. More experienced volunteers train and mentor newer ones to keep the program going and the offerings fresh. SJPL offers similar training for Reading to Children, a storytime alternative that stations volunteers in children's rooms for one-on-one reading to any interested child who drops in. The training includes how to select books that are good for reading aloud and how to read them in an engaging manner.

Still, volunteer programming is not without its potential challenges. Many volunteers are post-retirement, at an age where health problems or bad weather may keep them at home when they're scheduled to be at one of your branches. Make sure you have a backup plan in mind—perhaps a staff member who can jump in to provide that program or an alternative, but related one.

If you work in a union environment, the road to volunteer programming may be rocky. Many libraries under civil service or union rules specify that volunteers cannot do the jobs of paid staff; since library programming has traditionally been offered by librarians or assistants, you have a problem. Read your union and civil service rules carefully, and talk to union representatives as well as your administration. You will want to get buy-in from as many stakeholders as you can, just as you do with the bigger picture of centralized programming. Remember that there is a spectrum of volunteer programming rather than simply "yes, we do it" or "no, we don't." Some concessions you might agree to include the following:

- If a staff member has been doing a program, allowing them to keep doing so, not replacing them with a volunteer
- Not having volunteers do programs that only librarians generally do, but letting them provide non-librarian-level programs, or assist librarians who are running the program

- Not having volunteers do core programming, however you define that
- Limiting the number of programming hours done by volunteers to a certain percentage
- Allowing volunteers to do only programs that you wouldn't offer if there were no volunteers (e.g., you would not continue to offer résumé review service if your volunteer resigned)

Successful negotiation to allow volunteers to perform some programming can be hugely beneficial in terms of cost savings and community empowerment, but it might be hard on your central team. Two experiences with labor unions on this issue stand out for me. In one case, a union member attempted to intimidate me by coming into my office at night when everyone else had left to tell me that what I was trying to do (involving volunteers in programming) was illegal. In the other, a member of my central team was at a branch getting ready to set up for a program, and asked a union representative for the key to the room she'd reserved. The staff member was on her 15-minute break and refused to hand my librarian the key or to unlock the room for her until her break was up. This was certainly her legal right, but it demonstrated the hostility that some (not nearly all!) union representatives felt toward centralized programming in general, and volunteer programmers in particular.

PAID PERFORMERS

No matter how excellent your staff, how numerous your volunteers, how powerful your partnerships, sometimes you will want to hire a paid performer. Particularly for children's programs, there is a large array of high-quality programming available—from musicians to magicians to scientists to puppeteers. Your branches already know about local offerings and may have particular performers they hire on an annual basis, to kick off Summer Reading or celebrate Dia de los Muertos, for instance. One of the early jobs of your centralization project team could be to find out these local preferences and add their contact and pricing information to a central resource list.

The efficiency gained from centralization with regard to paid performers is that, as with partnerships, your central unit can make one phone call and book programs for all of your branches at once. Or, as we did at SJPL, you can make one phone call and learn the availability of the performer, and then add those slots as options on your programming menu.

If performers are paid by local Friends groups rather than from the library's budget, you may run into issues around local control. As difficult as change can be for library staff, it's often even harder for volunteers such as the Friends, who may not be able to understand why you refuse to let them have the same magician for Halloween that they've always had. This is one advantage to the resource list mentioned above—you can try to arrange your menus so that the magician is offered to everyone in October. But if 10 branches each have a different October favorite, you won't be able to please everyone. I found it most helpful to meet with Friends groups myself to explain that group bookings often resulted in discounts, which saved their hard-earned dollars, and that every branch had special favorites that we were trying our best to accommodate.

- Effective Parenting
- Physical and Emotional Well-Being
- Services to New Americans
- Support for Formal Education/Responsible Citizenship

In 2009, when an updated United Way report was released, we used those results to update our priorities, and then took them to a team of librarians and asked them to rename and regroup them so they'd be more intuitive for our staff. See Figure 8.1 for the document that was the result of this process.

CREATING THE MENU TEMPLATE

The menu is a critical document that your branches will need in order to make the right programming choices for their neighborhoods. In addition to the content of the menu—describing the programs you're offering—the document itself needs to be easy to use and comprehensive. It can be difficult to accomplish both!

In San José, we tried a number of different ways to present the menu options to the branches, tweaking as we went along, and heard feedback about what would help. At first, we sent each branch a simple spreadsheet (see Figure 8.1), with the programming priorities across the top and different types of program delivery down the left side. So, we would place a Music and Movement class, designed as a box program, in the Programs in a Box row and the Physical and Emotional Well-Being column. A branch that didn't want this program would simply delete it from the menu. A branch that did want it would leave that box filled in, and underneath it, they'd enter the day and time they planned to offer it.

As you can see from the figure, the two top rows of this early menu aren't exactly methods of program delivery like the other rows. Instead, they were Required Programming and City/Community Programs. Required Programs were what the project team had determined should be offered by every branch—storytime, teensReach (our teen volunteer group and advisory board), and Conversation Club (drop-in English-language conversation practice). These were listed in the top row so that it would be easy to verify that each branch had planned for these programs, and to underscore the importance of these consistent offerings system-wide.

The second row was for City/Community Programs. These refer to public events held at the branch by government agencies. As a municipal library, SJPL's usual sources for these programs were other city departments. For example, many branches hosted drop-in office hours for their local City Council representatives. Some branches had monthly Neighborhood Action

September Program Menu—Santa Teresa

	Cultural Traditions & Life Enrichment	Effective Parenting	Physical & Emotional Well Being	Reading Promotion	Services to New Americans	Support for Formal Education / Responsible Citizenship
Required programming: Every location provides these. Please state the days and times you will offer each of these *in italics*. For storytimes, also state whether it's aimed at baby, toddler, etc.	teens Reach meeting—1 per month. *4th Tuesday of each month From 4:00 P.M.–5:00 P.M.*			Storytime—3 per week *Wed: Toddler Storytime & Stay n Play 11:00 A.M.–12 noon, Family Storytime 6:30 P.M.; Thur: Preschool Storytime & Stay n Play 11:00 A.M.–12 noon*	Conversation Club—1 per week *Tuesdays 11–12*	
City and community programs: Programs offered by City and other government agencies like Councilmember office hours, NAC and			Coyote Creek Neighborhood Association Mtg. *September 15, 7:00 P.M.*	Friends book sale, *September 11, 10:00 A.M.–4:00 P.M.*		All-Friends Mtg *September 25, 9:30 A.M.–12 noon*

(Continued)

September Program Menu—Santa Teresa (*Continued*)

Cultural Traditions & Life Enrichment	Effective Parenting	Physical & Emotional Well Being	Reading Promotion	Services to New Americans	Support for Formal Education/ Responsible Citizenship
SNI meetings, Registrar of Voters. You will have all the programs listed. Please fill in the dates and times in *italics*. UPS-Presented Programs: Pick one per week. Please specify your preferred week/day/time and we will do our best to match it. Programs will be booked and scheduled by UPS. Delete any options you don't want this month.			Parent/Child Computer Class: Finding the Right Book for You (*2nd Thursday, afterschool*) 3PM		(1) Parent/Child Computer Class: Homework Resources (2) Parent/Child Computer Class: Online Safety and Privacy (3) Parent/Child Computer Class: Mousing and Typing for Beginners

(4) Parent/Child Computer Class: Searching the Library Catalog
(5) Getting Started with Email (for adults)
(6) Intro to Facebook (for teens and adults) *Sat 4th @ 1pm and Sat 25th @ 4 PM*
(7) Bubble Science for Kids *Fri 17th @ 3:30 PM*

Shaded boxes: Pick four per week. State the weeks/days/times you would like to offer these programs. For Programs in a Box and Staff-Presented Programs, your staff will present, so you can pick any days/times you want. For Partner-Presented Programs, please state your preferred dates/times and Innovation staff will schedule the programs. Delete any options you don't want this month.

| Programs in a Box | Autumn Fingerprint Tree Craft *Thurs 30th @ 3:00 P.M.* | Reading Readiness *Tues. 21st @ 6:30 P.M. Thur 23rd @ 3:00 P.M.* | (1) Wii Tournament for Teens *Sept. 10th and 24th, Fridays @ 4:00–5:30 P.M.* | Boatful of Pennies: Mixing in Math, ages 6–12 *Sat 25th @ 11:00 A.M.* |

(*Continued*)

September Program Menu—Santa Teresa (*Continued*)

	Cultural Traditions & Life Enrichment	Effective Parenting	Physical & Emotional Well Being	Reading Promotion	Services to New Americans	Support for Formal Education / Responsible Citizenship
Staff Programs						
Partner-Presented Programs						
Volunteer-Presented Programs: State the weeks/days/times you will offer these programs. Pick as many per week as you can support with projected staffing levels. You will contact and schedule the volunteers for each program. Delete any options you don't want to offer this month.	Chess Class *Tues. Weekly 6:00–7:30 P.M. except for 9/28.* Friends' Booksale *Sat. Sept 11th 10:00 A.M.–5:00 P.M.*			(1) *Reading to Children (all weekly) Tues: 11:00 A.M.–12 noon and 6:00–7:00 P.M., Thurs. 4:30–5:30 P.M.* (2) *Our Book Club Every 3rd Wednesday 7:00–8:00 P.M. "Me Talk Pretty One Day" title for Sept.*	*Lawyer in the Library, Maki Kanayama Sat, Sept. 4, 18, 25, 10:00 A.M.–12 noon*	Homework Club *(Weekly) Wed. 3:30–5:30 P.M. (follow-ing computer info is Weekly):* Open Computer Lab Tuesdays *12 noon–1:00 P.M., and Wed 2:00–4:00 P.M. and 5:00–7:00 P.M., and Thurs. 11:00 A.M.–1:00 P.M.*

Young Inklings: Writing Class for Children ($225) *Tues. 28th @ 6:30 P.M. to?*

Friends-Sponsored Performers: Pick one per month IF your Friends would like to pay for it and you have staff to support it. Specify your preferred week/day/time and we will do our best to match it. Programs will be booked and scheduled by UPS. Delete the options you don't want this month.

Week 1	Sept. 1–4
Week 2	Sept. 5–11
Week 3	Sept. 12–18
Week 4	Sept. 19–25
Week 5	Sept. 26–Oct. 2

Figure 8.1   An early programming menu from San José Public Library

Committee meetings, or hosted the Mayor's Gang Prevention Task Force Summit. Most branches had local Friends of the Library groups, and their book sales and membership meetings were also included in this row of the menu. These arrangements were handled locally; when we sent the branches their menus, this row was left blank for them to fill in, based on their own schedules.

The third row on the early program menu was used for centrally presented programs. Branches were asked to choose one program per week for the central team to present in person. They would delete the programs they didn't want, and for the ones they did, they would list their preferred days and times. Since we had to schedule our four librarians among 19 locations, it was more helpful when branches listed "any Tuesday between 3:00 P.M. and 4:30 P.M." or "any Saturday morning," rather than giving specific days and times.

Row four listed Programs in a Box. Since the branch staff were presenting these programs themselves, without the need for a central librarian to visit, they could choose any day or time that worked for them. The only restriction was that they had to stay within the target numbers (of programs) developed by the project team.

Row five was used for locally developed programs. Again, since these did not require central staff, local staff could choose their own days and times. However, for each row five program they picked, they had to eliminate a row four program in order to stay within their target numbers. At this point, you may be asking yourself why locally presented programming has a place in a completely centralized library! The answer is that during the first year, when centralization was such a huge change for librarians, we wanted to allow some flexibility. In some cases, there were long-time local favorite program series, and to end them abruptly would have been a customer disservice. The intent was for branches to transition these to volunteer-led programs. In other cases, the quality of the local programming was quite high, and we wanted the branch creating it to turn it into a Program in a Box that could be offered centrally in the future.

The sixth row covered partner-presented programming that was coordinated centrally. As with the third row, branches provided their preferred days and times, and we did our best to schedule within these whenever possible.

Row seven was used for volunteer-run programs, handled at the local level. Like with row five, the staff filled in the programs, dates, and times themselves.

The eighth and final row included paid performers, usually sponsored by branches' local Friends groups. These were coordinated centrally and offered on the same basis as central and partner programming.

After the first month, the feedback we heard was that the menu wasn't enough. Before choosing programs, local staff wanted to read fuller descriptions of the programs, including topics covered, age group, price, if applicable, setup needed, and more. We listened to our internal customers and responded with a document called "What the Heck is That Program?" (Figure 8.2 shows the first page of this). This detailed list gave all the information we had on each program we were offering, and could be reached by just a click from our revised menu (Figure 8.3). We kept this format for the first year of centralization.

After nine or ten months of centralized programming, there were so many virtual box programs that they were threatening to take over the entire menu. At that point, rather than continuing to squeeze long lists into the documents, we began to only showcase new or seasonal virtual box programs via the menu. We added a note saying that the back catalog was still available for selection each month, and could be viewed on our intranet site.

The next year, the menu was changed to reflect further feedback from front-line staff. The "What the Heck is That Program?" document was merged into the menu, making one long document instead of two shorter linked ones (Figure 8.4). Instead of having to enter ongoing programs such as storytime each month, these dates and times were simply communicated once to the clerical staff, who then created calendar database entries for the entire year. The central unit provided forms that the branch staff could fill out (electronically, of course) if one of these programs changed. They also switched to a bimonthly format instead of monthly, which meant that outside performers could be scheduled over a longer time period, making it more likely that everyone who wanted to hire the performer could have the chance.

Rest assured, your program menu will be different! Perhaps instead of topical categories along the top of your menu, you'd like to see age levels or other target audiences (Spanish speakers, job seekers, etc.). Maybe you won't have any local programming during your first year, or maybe you'll shoot for 50 percent local. The spreadsheet format, though, will allow you to see at a glance where the gaps are, for both your central offerings and the branches' eventual choices.

MENU ALTERNATIVES

If you're not moving to full centralization, there are other options you can choose for streamlining your programming without creating full monthly menus. You could simply rotate storytime boxes, for example (see Chapter 5). You could also create other box programs that follow rotations similar to storytime boxes.

WHAT THE HECK IS THAT PROGRAM? OR, DESCRIPTIONS OF CENTRALIZED PROGRAMMING FOR FEBRUARY/MARCH 2011

UPS-Delivered Programs

Before You Buy: Fine Jewelry

Are you planning to buy fine jewelry for your loved one for Valentine's Day or for a special birthday? This class will help you find information to inform this large ticket purchase by accessing Consumer Reports on our website for up to date information.

Create Your Own Family Mini Quilt of Memories

We provide the materials, you provide the memories. This is a family activity designed to involve everyone. Quilt will be something like this but details are to be determined in a few weeks: http://bit.ly/h9doaU

Make a Mural for the San José Children's Faire

UPS staff will come with supplies for a mural and help your kids get it done! The theme this year is: Play together, Learn together, Growing with Giggles and Grins! This is a perfect free craft and the kids will get to go see their art in April at the Children's Faire for Month of the Young Child.

Making Musical Instruments

Elementary-school aged children will have a musical blast building musical instruments using readymade kits from RAFT with our UPS librarians. We'll make The Glove-a-Phone and/or the Tongue Depressor Harmonica.

Mixing in Math: Card Games

A UPS librarian will go to your branch and set up a table with two or three "mixing in math" activities for children to participate in, including math related card games. These will be "walk by and try" activities

Figure 8.2   San José Public Library's program description document

where not all children need to participate at the same time. This program is best suited to after school, or another time when many children are coming and going in the library. Please have a table and chair ready for the UPS staff person in a well-trafficked part of the library. Please note that these are new mixing in math activities (the ones from previous months are available as a programs in a box).

Nature Talks by Open Space Authority

Offered by popular demand! Programs on bears, wolves, mushrooms, wildflowers and butterflies, and newts and salamanders are all possibilities. Almaden Branch has already requested the first Tuesday of each month for February and March. Rave review from AB—Pam Crider says, "I just wanted to share with you how pleased we were with last evening's Mysterious Mountain Lion program, presented by Interpreter Teri Rogoway. This event was truly a family program, enjoyed by children and adults alike, as opposed to a program aimed at the kids that adults tolerate! Ms. Rogoway kept all 20 participants engaged in the presentation." Please state which topic you want, and your second choice too.

Figure 8.2 (*Continued*)

January 2011 Program Menu—West Valley

Week 1 Jan. 2–8
Week 2 Jan. 9–15
Week 3 Jan. 16–22
Week 4 Jan. 24–29

Instructions for This Month

1. Fill in the # of calendars you want us to order: 400
2. **BOLD** any programs below you want UPS to make fliers for. We will automatically make fliers for any programs in the blue, yellow, green, and Programs in a Box lines, so you don't have to bold those.
3. Put an ASTERISK * next to any programs for which you want to thank the Friends on your calendar.
4. List all blurbs for your LOCAL programs at the bottom of the menu. Blurbs not on the menu will not be included on the back of your calendar, and no flier can be made without a blurb. Not needed if there was a blurb on your December calendar. Not needed for the programs planned centrally.

FOR PROGRAM DESCRIPTIONS, click here: http://bit.ly/9b5Bds

Cultural Traditions & Life Enrichment	Effective Parenting	Physical & Emotional Well Being	Reading Promotion	Services to New Americans	Support for Formal Education / Responsible Citizenship
teens Reach meeting—1 per month—Week 3 Thurs 4:00–5:00 P.M.		inclusive ST—1 per month—week 3 Sat 2:00–2:30 P.M.	Storytime—4 per week—Bilingual Jpn-Eng ST (w/ Kazuko): Wednesdays 11:00 A.M.; Family ST / Stay & Play: Wednesdays 6:00 P.M.; Lapsit ST / Stay & Play: Thursdays 11:00 A.M.; Family ST / Stay & Play: Saturdays 11:00 A.M.	Conversation Club—1 per week—Tuesdays 6:30–7:30 P.M.	

Required programming: Every location provides these. Please state the days and times you will offer each of these. For storytimes, also state whether it's baby, toddler, etc.

City and community programs: Programs offered by City and other government agencies like Councilmember office hours, NAC and SNI meetings, Friends meetings/sales, etc. Please add week/day/time info. Delete any programs no longer offered, and add any that we missed.			Friends of the Library Meeting and Potluck Week 3 Sat 10:00 A.M.	1. District 1 Councilmember Pete Constant holds open office hours Week 1 Wed 6:30 P.M.
UPS-Presented Programs: Pick one per week. Please specify your preferred week/day/time and we will do our best to match it. Programs will be booked and scheduled by UPS. Fill in your choices in the week lines below.	1. "I Have a Dream" craft 2. South Bay Guitar Society	Puppet Making for Families	1. Open Space Authority ecoProach 2. Green Talk	1. Before You Buy: Exercise Machine 2. Mixing in Math: Narrow It Down 3. Computer Basics: Internet

(Continued)

January 2011 Program Menu—West Valley (*Continued*)

	Cultural Traditions & Life Enrichment	Effective Parenting	Physical & Emotional Well Being	Reading Promotion	Services to New Americans	Support for Formal Education / Responsible Citizenship
Week 1–Jan. 2–8	1. Dream (2nd choice) Sat 2:00 P.M.					2. MiM—W, Th or F after 3:00 P.M.
Week 2–Jan. 9–15	1. Dream (1st choice) Sat 2:00 P.M.	(2nd choice) Sat 2:00 P.M.				
Week 3–Jan. 16–22			1. Open Space (1st choice) Tues 6:00 P.M.			
Week 4–Jan. 23–29		(1st choice) Sat 2:00 P.M.	1. Open Space (2nd choice) Tues 6:00 P.M.			

Shaded boxes: Pick your allotted number per week. Local staff will present, so you can pick any days/times you want. Enter them in the spaces for the individual weeks. Don't forget to pick a day and time.

PROGRAMS IN A BOX				
1. Teen Crafts 2. Sports & News Online 3. Calendar Bingo	Reading Readiness in English or Spanish	1. Wii Tournament for Teens and/or Children 2. Music and Movement 3. Snack Smart	1. Book Adventures 2. Smokey the Bear storytime	1. Parent/Child Computer Class 2. Putting Your Photos Online 3. Before You Buy: Digital Cameras 4. Intro to Facebook 5. Getting Started with Email 6. Basic Typing and Mousing 7. Before You Buy: TV
Week 1—Jan. 2–8				
Week 2—Jan. 9–15				
Week 3—Jan. 16–22		1. Wii Wed 3:30 P.M.*		
Week 4—Jan. 23–29	3. Calendar Bingo Tues 4:00 P.M.			5. email Thurs 1:00 P.M.

(*Continued*)

January 2011 Program Menu—West Valley (*Continued*)

	Cultural Traditions & Life Enrichment	Effective Parenting	Physical & Emotional Well Being	Reading Promotion	Services to New Americans	Support for Formal Education / Responsible Citizenship
STAFF PROGRAMS			Legos @ The Library Week 1, 2, 3, 4 Fri 4:00–5:00 P.M.	West Valley Book Club Week 2 Wed 6:30 P.M.		
Week 1—Jan. 2–8			Legos @ The Library Fri 4:00–5:00 P.M.			
Week 2—Jan. 9–15			Legos @ The Library Fri 4:00–5:00 P.M.	West Valley Book Club Wed 6:30 P.M.		
Week 3—Jan. 16–22			Legos @ The Library Fri 4:00–5:00 P.M.			
Week 4—Jan. 23–29			Legos @ The Library Fri 4:00–5:00 P.M.			
Local Volunteer- and Partner-Presented Programs: State the weeks/days/times	Anime Club for Teens Weeks 1, 3, Fri 4:00–5:30 P.M.; Master.			1. Reading to Rover (partner: Canine Companions) Week 3 Thurs 3:30–5:00 P.M.		1. One-on-One Computer Help (Greg) All Weeks

you will offer these programs. Work out the details with the volunteer or existing partner individually. (Any new partnerships should be referred to UPS insteadt) Pick as many per week as you can support with projected staffing levels. Delete any options you don't want to offer this month.	Gardeners Week 4 Wed 6:30–8:00 P.M	2. Reading Buddies All weeks, Tues 4–5pm and Sat 11:30 A.M.– 12:30 P.M.	Tues 5:00–6:00 P.M. 2. One-on-One Computer Help (Maggi) All Weeks, Thurs 4:00–6:00 P.M. 3. Homework Hour All Weeks, Tues 5:00–6:00 P.M. AND Thurs 5:00–6:00 P.M.
Friends-Sponsored Performers: Pick as many per month as your staffing levels and your Friends can support. Specify your preferred weeks/days/times and we will do our best to	1. Baby Sign Language* any Thurs 11:00 A.M. (in place of story time)		

(Continued)

January 2011 Program Menu—West Valley (*Continued*)

Cultural Traditions & Life Enrichment	Effective Parenting	Physical & Emotional Well Being	Reading Promotion	Services to New Americans	Support for Formal Education / Responsible Citizenship
match them, but cannot guarantee. Programs will be booked and scheduled by UPS. Delete the options you don't want this month.					

Blurbs:

Master Gardeners Week 4 Wed 6:30–8PM

Learn from Master Gardener Allen Buchinski how to prune different types of fruit trees for structure, shape and fruit production. Allen volunteers his skill at the Emma Prusch Park Farm's High Density Fruit Orchard where the trees are kept small and at a reduced height to make harvesting ladder-free!

Figure 8.3   San José Public Library's program menu

January Programming Menu for Insert Name Here Branch

Please order insert number English calendars; insert number Spanish calendars (if needed)

High Priority Programs:

Program Title	Stay & Play?	Room	Beginning Date	Repeats		Start Time	Ending Date
Baby and Toddler Storytime (Parenting)	choose yes or no	Choose a room	Click here to enter a date.	Weekly Choose a day			Click here to enter a date.
Preschool Storytime (Literacy)	choose yes or no	Choose a room	Click here to enter a date.	Weekly Choose a day			Click here to enter a date.
Family Storytime (Literacy)	choose yes or no	Choose a room	Click here to enter a date.	Weekly Choose a day			Click here to enter a date.
Inclusive Storytime (Health)	choose yes or no	Choose a room	Click here to enter a date.	Choose a week of the month	Choose a day		Click here to enter a date.
Conversation Club (Literacy)		Choose a room	Click here to enter a date.	Weekly Choose a day			Click here to enter a date.
teensReach Meeting (Community)		Choose a room	Click here to enter a date.	Choose a week of the month	Choose a day		Click here to enter a date.

Notes: (i.e. Inclusive storytime replaces preschool storytime on 11/2, Preschool Storytime on Tuesdays is Bilingual English/Spanish).

Figure 8.4   A menu used in the second year of centralization at San José Public Library

City and Community Programs:

Program Title	Beginning Date	Time	Program Repeats:		
Friends Meeting (Community)	Click here to enter a date.		Choose frequency	Choose a day of the week	Choose a week of the month
Description for Web Events Here					
NAC Meeting (Community)	Click here to enter a date.		Choose frequency	Choose a day of the week	Choose a week of the month
Description for Web Events Here					
Council members public hours (Community)	Click here to enter a date.		Choose frequency	Choose a day of the week	Choose a week of the month
Description for Web Events Here					
Friends Booksale (Literacy)	Click here to enter a date.		Choose frequency	Choose a day of the week	Choose a week of the month
Description for Web Events Here					
Program Title (Service Area)	Click here to enter a date.		Choose frequency	Choose a day of the week	Choose a week of the month
Description for Web Events Here					

Notes:

Figure 8.4 (Continued)

UPS Programs: **You may choose 3 programs delivered by UPS staff or partner agencies.**

Program Title	Location/Attendance Limits	First Choice Dates/times	Second Choice Dates/times
eReader Petting Zoo (Literacy)	Community Room	Click here to enter a date.	Click here to enter a date.
	Adults	Start time:	Start time:
Description: IDEAS staff will deliver this program. The program will include the opportunity to meet the Kindle, Sony Reader, iPad, and other devices for e-Reading. IDEAS staff will talk about different e-collections at the library, and show customers how easy it is to get free library eBooks on their device! This drop-in program will last 2 hours, and patrons are welcome to bring their own smartphone or eReader device to follow along. **Availability:** This program is available on Tuesdays, Wednesdays, and Fridays and must finish before 3:00 or Saturday 1/28 all day. **Prep Time/Duties:** Please have a staff person available to help with the program and have the space set up 30 minutes prior to program start time. **Space/Equipment Needs:** This program can be held anywhere as long as few tables are set up and there is a power outlet nearby. **Public Blurb:** Meet the Kindle, Sony Reader, iPad, and other devices for e-Reading! We'll talk about all the different e-collections at the library, and show you how easy it is to get free library eBooks on your device! Did you get a new eReader over the holidays? You're welcome to bring your own smartphone or eReader device to follow along. This drop-in demonstration will last for 2 hours.			
SAT or ACT practice test with Kaplan: (Literacy)	Community Room	Click here to enter a date.	Click here to enter a date.
	Teens	Start time:	Start time:
Description: A representative from KAPLAN will go to your branch and proctor a full length SAT or ACT test. This 4 hour practice test gives students a chance to take a 'real' SAT or ACT test, and receive their results via e-mail. The best dates for SAT practice tests would be Jan 7th or Jan 21st. Jan 14th is in the middle of a 3-day weekend and on Jan 28th is an official SAT test date. **Please specify on your Menu if you want the SAT or ACT test.** **Prep Time/Duties:** Post flyer, promote to local youth groups and schools, Set up room for test. **Space/Equipment Needs:** Please supply chairs and tables in an enclosed room (such as FLC or Community Room). **Public blurb:** Find out how you would score on the _____. Take a full length practice _____ test, proctored by KAPLAN. This is a great opportunity to try your hand at the types of questions you will see on the actual test. The test lasts just over 4 hours and is open to all high school students. Pre-Registration is required.			

Figure 8.4   (*Continued*)

81

Math Fun: Fun with Fractions (Literacy)	Children's area of the library	Click here to enter a date.	Click here to enter a date.
		Start time:	Start time:

Description: A UPS librarian will come to your branch to lead fun math activities. Ages: 5-12 years old.
Availability: You choose when you what us to come to you!
Prep Time/Duties: Please have the space set up 30 minutes prior to program start time.
Space/Equipment Needs: A table and chairs stationed in a high traffic area or Children's area would be best.
Public Blurb: Math Fun: Fun with Fractions! Children ages 5 to 12 are invited to explore fractions with fun math activities.

Firebird Youth Chinese Orchestra (Culture)	Choose a room	Click here to enter a date.	Click here to enter a date.
		Start time:	Start time:

Description: The Firebird Youth Chinese Orchestra (FYCO) is offering two free 45-minute performances.
Availability: Saturday, 1/28 and Saturday, 2/4 @ 2pm.
Prep Time/Duties: They need one hour prep time.
Space/Equipment Needs: 20 chairs for the musicians + chairs for audience.
Public Blurb: Celebrate the new year with a magical performance by the Firebird Youth Chinese Orchestra. Enjoy this fantastic concert comprised of traditional Chinese instruments.

Lunar New Year Craft (Culture)	Choose a room	Click here to enter a date.	Click here to enter a date.
		Start time:	Start time:

Description: A UPS librarian will come to your branch to share a Lunar New Year craft with your customers.
Availability: You choose when you what us to come to you!
Prep Time/Duties: Please have the space set up 30 minutes prior to program start time.
Space/Equipment Needs: Plenty of tables and chairs in your Family Place or in the Community Room.
Public Blurb: Celebrate Lunar New Year with your library. Create a Lunar New Year Craft. Have fun with your friends.

Figure 8.4 (*Continued*)

		Choose a room	Click here to enter a date.	Click here to enter a date.
Conflict Resolution Workshop for teensReach (Community)		teensReach members	Start time:	Start time:

Description: A UPS librarians will attend your teensReach meeting and conduct a conflict resolution workshop as part of your teensReach meeting. The workshop will take about 45 minutes. **Please schedule this program during your teensReach meeting** This program will also be offered in February.
Prep Time/Duties: Notify teensReach members about upcoming meeting.
Space/Equipment Needs: Colored markers.

		Choose a room	Click here to enter a date	Click here to enter a date
Green Waste Recovery Inc. (Community) Here's a link to obtain further information and details about the plastic bag ban. http://www.sfrecycles.org/bags/retailers.asp			Start time:	Start time:

Description: Green Waste will host an informational table and ESD will provide recycle bags for the customers to take home.
Availability: TBD
Prep Time/Duties: Please have a staff person assigned to greet/interface with the partner and have the space set up 30 minutes prior to program start time. Please promote this event by word of mouth. Post flyer, promote event, set up room, welcome presenter.
Space/Equipment Needs: A table and chairs stationed in a high traffic area will be best.
Public Blurb: Stop by the library to learn more about the plastic bag ban. Green Waste will be on hand to answer your questions.

	Choose a room		Click here to enter a date.	Click here to enter a date.
Puzzle Fun at Your Library **(Community)**			Start time:	Start time:

Description: Jan. 29 is National Puzzle Day, but we can celebrate all month long! Have a UPS librarian come to your branch to celebrate Nation Puzzle Day with your younger customers.
Availability: You choose when you what us to come to you!
Prep Time/Duties: Please have the space set up 30 minutes prior to program start time.
Space/Equipment Needs: Plenty of tables and chairs in your Family Place or in the Community Room
Public Blurb: Celebrate National Puzzle Day with your library. Play with puzzles and crosswords and more! Fun for all.

Figure 8.4 *(Continued)*

Pathways: **Nutrition For Healthy Aging (Health)**		Choose a room	Click here to enter a date.	Click here to enter a date.
		Limited to community room/space size.	Start time:	Start time:

Description: Pathways not-for-profit agency will present these programs free of charge. They need to fulfill their outreach mission tool
Prep Time/Duties: Please talk to presenter prior to workshop, and check on the workshop periodically.
Space/Equipment Needs: A room with a projector and laptop. A community room is best, but if a portable projector is available, another space can be used.

Puppet Making for Families **(Parenting)**	Community room or Children's Area	Click here to enter a date.	Click here to enter a date.
	Children and Parents	Start time:	Start time:

Description: This make-and-take workshop (presented by the UPS librarians) for parents and children will include puppet making, tips for parent on the use of puppets, and an interactive story reading where the children can use the puppets they created. All handouts will be in English and Spanish.
Prep Time/Duties: Post flyer, promote event, set up tables and chairs
Space/Equipment Needs: Scissors, crayons, Tables and chairs.
Public Blurb: Puppets are a wonderful way to help children learn language, and help parents to get their child through daily routines (such as dressing or cleaning up). In this workshop for parents and children ages 3 to 7, we will make puppets and use them to tell a story.

Am I Ready to Start a Small Business? **(Finance)**		Choose a room	Click here to enter a date.	Click here to enter a date.
		Limited to room size	Start time:	Start time:

Description: An experienced speaker from SCORE (Service Corps of Retired Executives) will talk about what it takes to start a small business. Talks are usually 40 min. with 20 min or so for questions.
Availability: Prefer M-F daytime, Evenings & Saturdays maybe. First two branches to respond. Please pick top 2 dates/times.
Space/Equipment Needs Community Room or Group Study Room. Powerpoint use depends on speaker but usually not used.
Prep Time/Duties: Promotion. Room set-up. Powerpoint use depends on speaker but usually not used.

Business Plans **(Finance)**		Choose a room	Click here to enter a date.	Click here to enter a date.
			Start time:	Start time:

Description: An experienced speaker from SCORE (Service Corps of Retired Executives) will talk about all you need to know about writing a business plan. Talks are usually 40 min. with 20 min. or so for questions.
Availability: Prefer M-F daytime, Evenings & Saturdays maybe. First two branches to respond. Please pick top 2 dates/times.
Space/Equipment Needs Community Room or Group Study Room. Powerpoint use depends on speaker but usually not used.
Prep Time/Duties: Promotion. Room set-up. Powerpoint use depends on speaker but usually not used.

Figure 8.4 (*Continued*)

Credit Myths, ID Theft, or Access to Capital for Small Businesses provided by Greg Meyer of Meriwest Credit Union (please pick one and indicate choice in notes) (Finance)	Storytime area or community room	Community Room	Click here to enter a date. Start time:
		Limited to Community Room size.	

Description: Greg Meyer will speak about Credit Myths.

Availability: TBD

Prep Time/Duties: Please have a staff person assigned to greet/interface with the partner and have the space set up 30 minutes prior to program start time.

Space/Equipment Needs: A table and chairs stationed in a high traffic area or the community room will be best.

Public Blurb:

Credit Myths & Repair w/ Greg Meyer or associate. "Learn the top ten myths of credit and how to access and initiate corrections to your credit report."

Social Security in the Library (Community)	Choose a room	Click here to enter a date. Start time:	Click here to enter a date. Start time:

Description: Social Security will host a table at your library to answer questions about benefits.

Availability: TBD

Prep Time/Duties: Please have a staff person assigned to greet/interface with the partner and have the space set up 30 minutes prior to program start time.

Space/Equipment Needs: A table and chairs stationed in a high traffic area will be best.

Public Blurb: Are you ready to file for Retirement or Medicare benefits online? This workshop provides individuals an opportunity to discuss filing online with a Social Security Representative while saving you a trip to your Social Security office. No appointment necessary, walk-ins welcome. For specific questions you will need to bring the following documents with you: Social Security Number, Birth record if born outside of the US, Last year's W-9 or tax return, and Bank account information for direct deposit. If you have additional questions, call the local Social Security office at 866-331-2235.

Figure 8.4   (*Continued*)

Programs in a Box

Program Title	Date	Start Time	Where?	Registration?	Repeats?
Calendar Craft & Bingo (Culture)	Click here to enter a date.	Starts:	Choose a room	No preregistration required	no repeat

Description: Get ready for 2012! This program in a virtual box features bingo cards with the year's holidays instead of numbers and letters. Children can also decorate a twelve-month calendar to display at home, and fill in their birthdays and other important family events. The materials in the virtual box will be updated for 2012, and in addition, you will receive small bingo prizes (eg. Pencils, stickers, etc)

Cost/Supplies/Equipment: You will need crayons or markers and any other craft supplies your branch has on hand to decorate the calendars.

Space Needs: Tables/chairs for participants.   Preparation Time/Duties: Post flyer, promote event, set up room, print out calendar templates.

Public Blurb: Create a calendar for the new year, at this fun event for the whole family. We will be decorating calendars with a variety of art supplies, and celebrating the coming year with a fun game of bingo.

Advanced Craft: Monster Making (Culture)	Click here to enter a date.	Starts:	Choose a room	No preregistration required	no repeat

Description: Receive a box of supplies for teens and tweens to make felt monsters. Supplies will include felt, stuffing, buttons, string and more.

Cost/Supplies/Equipment: The branch should provide scissors, and pencils.

Preparation Time/Duties: post flyer, promote event to teens, make a sample to get familiar with supplies, host event for about 1 hour

Attendance Limits: If you expect more than 20 teens/tweens, please contact Aleta for additional supplies.

Public Blurb: Let your creativity loose and take home a unique felt monster! Teens and tweens are invited to learn to sew with this fun craft activity. Bring your friends and join in the fun! All supplies will be provided.

Battle of the Bands 2012: Recording Session (Culture)	Click here to enter a date.	Starts:	Choose a room	Yes Preregistraion is required	no repeat

Description: Battle of the Bands is back for 2012! This year we will have an added component to the contest: we will judge the quality of the videos the bands submit and give a prize for the best video. It will now be even more important for the bands to put some effort into making a good video. The winner of the video contest will be announced during Teen Tech Week.

Host a recording session at your branch: staff member assists bands in recording one song. Bands have to bring their equipment, the branch provides the space (community room), the flip camera and the laptop for upload to youtube. Staff member assists with filming and uploading the video.

Public Blurb: Battle of the Bands is back! All teen bands are encouraged to sign up for our annual contest. This year we will also be giving out a prize for the best video submitted for the contest. Still need to shoot that video? Don't have the space / equipment? Sign up for our recording session!

Preparation Time/Duties: post flyer, promote event to teens, prepare room, host event

Celebrate Dr. King's Birthday with a Craft (Community)	Click here to enter a date.	Starts:	Choose a room	No preregistration required	no repeat

Description: Celebrate Dr. King's Birthday with fun from this virtual craft box. Please let us know if you need supplies for the craft.

Prep Time/Duties: Post flyer, promote event to children/families, prepare room, host event.

Public Blurb: Celebrate the Birthday of Dr. Martin Luther King, Jr. by making a beautiful craft. Talk about Dr. King's legacy, his dreams, and enjoy making a craft

Figure 8.4   (*Continued*)

with your children.

Environmental Craft: Decorate a Bag (Community)	Click here to enter a date.	Starts:	Choose a room	**No preregistration required**	no repeat

Description: In January the 'plastic bag ban' will go into effect in the city of San Jose. In this craft activity teens and tweens will decorate a reusable bag with fabric paint. During the craft the staff member can talk to the participant's about the importance of using reusable bags and the impact plastic bags have on the environment. Agenda and supporting documents are available on SharePoint. Canvas bags and fabric paint will be provided by UPS.

Cost/Supplies/Equipment: The branch should provide table coverings.

Public Blurb: Teens and tweens: Decorate a shopping bag at this fun craft activity. Join us with your friends! All supplies provided.

Preparation Time/Duties: post flyer, promote event to teens and tweens make a sample to get familiar with supplies, host event for about 1 hour

Attendance Limits: If you expect more than 20 teens/tweens, please contact Birgit for additional supplies.

Apply Now! (Finance)	Click here to enter a date.	Starts:	Tech Center	**No preregistration required**	no repeat

Description: Use the resources of Career Transitions to apply for jobs that suit your skills and interests, secure an interview and even practice interview techniques.

Cost/Supplies/Equipment: Uses Career Transitions and resources provided by Gale and found on Sharepoint: Programming Services > ComputerClasses Box.

Preparation Time/Duties: post flyer, promote event Review resources provided online. Attendance Limits: Available work stations in computer lab

Public blurb: Be prepared for your next job interview.

Choose older programs in a box by filling in these spaces	Click here to enter a date.	Starts:	Choose a room	**No preregistration required**	no repeat
Description:					
			Other (specify in Notes)	**No preregistration required**	no repeat
Description:					
			Other (specify in Notes)	**No preregistration required**	no repeat
Description:					
			Other (specify in Notes)	**No preregistration required**	no repeat
Description:					
			Other (specify in Notes)	**No preregistration required**	no repeat
Description:					

Notes: Program Room

Figure 8.4 (*Continued*)

Volunteer and Partner Programs (planned locally)

Title	Date	Start time	Registration?	Repeats?	Where?	Exceptions	End Date
Title	Click here to enter a date.	Start time:	No preregistration required	Choose Day of Week	Choose a room	Click here to enter a date.	Click here to enter a date.
Service Area				Choose Frequency			
Enter Description for web events here:							
Title	Click here to enter a date.	Start time:	No preregistration required	Choose Day of Week	Choose a room	Click here to enter a date.	Click here to enter a date.
Service Area				Choose Frequency			
Enter Description for web events here:							
Title	Click here to enter a date.	Start time:	No preregistration required	Choose Day of Week	Choose a room	Click here to enter a date.	Click here to enter a date.
Service Area				Choose Frequency			
Enter Description for web events here:							
Title	Click here to enter a date.	Start time:	No preregistration required	Choose Day of Week	Choose a room	Click here to enter a date.	Click here to enter a date.
Service Area				Choose Frequency			
Enter Description for web events here:							
Title	Click here to enter a date.	Start time:	No preregistration	Choose Day of Week	Choose a room	Click here to enter a date.	Click here to enter a date.

Figure 8.4 (*Continued*)

Service Area	date.		required	Choose Frequency			
Enter Description for web events here:							
Title	Click here to enter a date.	**Start time:**	**No preregistration required**	Choose Day of Week	**Choose a room**	Click here to enter a date.	Click here to enter a date.
Service Area				weekly			
Enter Description for web events here:							
Title	Click here to enter a date.	**Start time:**	**No preregistration required**	Choose Day of Week	**Choose a room**	Click here to enter a date.	Click here to enter a date.
Service Area				Choose Frequency			
Enter Description for web events here:							
Title	Click here to enter a date.	**Start time:**	**No preregistration required**	Choose Day of Week	**Choose a room**	Click here to enter a date.	Click here to enter a date.
Service Area				Choose Frequency			
Enter Description for web events here:							

Notes:

Figure 8.4 (*Continued*)

89

Paid performers: Use Available Friends or Gift Trust Funds

Performer	1st Choice Date	1st Choice Time	2nd Choice Date	2nd Choice Time	Room
Mad Science (Literacy) **Price:** $250 for single performance, multiple performances: $150.	Click here to enter a date.	Start time:	Click here to enter a date.	Start time:	Entrance area (marketplace)
Description: Mad Science® is the world's leading science enrichment provider. They deliver unique, live science experiences for children that are as entertaining as they are educational. Mad Science encourages scientific literacy in children in an age when science is as vital as reading, writing and arithmetic. **Availability:** Currently fully available for Saturday and weekday mornings. **Prep Time/Duties:** Please have a staff person assigned to help with the program and have the space set up 30 minutes prior to program start time. **Space/Equipment Needs:** Community Room **Public Blurb:** Mad Science makes learning about science as fun as it is educational! See mad scientists perform exciting, interactive experiments the whole family will enjoy.					
Author Oliver Chin: The Year of the Dragon (Literacy)	Click here to enter a date.	Start time:	Click here to enter a date.	Start time:	Community Room
Description: Author Oliver Chin will go to your branch and give a talk/reading and give a presentation about Chinese New Year, then he will read the story (and show a PDF of the illustrations on the projector). Lastly children will do Zodiac animal themed coloring sheets (Branch would need to provide crayons and photo copies). Please make sure that there is someone from your Friends group who can sell the books for him (they would get a 10% cut). Cost: $150 Preparation Time/Duties: post flyer, promote event, set up room with laptop and projector, welcome performer Attendance Limits: For children.					
Charles the Clown (Culture) **Price:** $100.	Click here to enter a date.	Start time:	Click here to enter a date.	Start time:	Entrance area (marketplace)
Description: Charles The Clown is the clown you should have if you have children or people afraid of clowns in the audience. Charles puts his make-up and costume on so that everyone can see that there is a real man inside all the frippery. **Availability:** Charles appreciates the opportunity to do two shows in one day and is available: January 2, 3, 4, 5, 6, 9, 10, 13, 14 (after 1:30 pm)16, 17, 23, 24, 25, 26, 27, 30, 31. February 2, 3, 4. (He could take three shows on Saturday, Feb 4th, pending drive time being sufficient) **Prep Time/Duties:** Please have a staff person assigned to help with the program and have the space set up 30 minutes prior to program start time. **Space/Equipment Needs:** Community Room **Public Blurb:** Watch Charles The Clown, award winning entertainer and recording artist, perform his hilarious become-a-clown routine. The show features Biscuit The Dog Puppet, balloon antics, silly magic and comic rhyming that makes the performance a language-rich experience.					
Jaliya (Culture) **Price: TBD (approx. $200-$400)**	Click here to enter a date.	Start time:	Click here to enter a date.	Start time:	Entrance area (marketplace)
Description: David Piper and his crew will come to wow you with his drumming and a doll craft **Availability:** TBD **Prep Time/Duties:** Please have a staff person assigned to greet/interface with the performers and have the space set up 30 minutes prior to program start time. Volunteers to help with the craft would be ideal. **Space/Equipment Needs:** Plenty of tables and chairs					

Figure 8.4   (*Continued*)

Public Blurb: Join Jaliya and Friends to enjoy their rhythmic drumming. Then learn how to make a doll to take home. Ages five and up.

Menlo Brass Quartet (Culture) **Price: $750**	Click here to enter a date.	Start time:	Click here to enter a date.	Start time:	Entrance area (marketplace)

Description: The Menlo Brass Quintet enjoys a reputation as one of the San Francisco Bay Area's finest brass quintets, renowned for outstanding musicianship and the unparalleled diversity of their repertoire featuring more than 1,000 compositions, including over 100 original pieces, performed for the enjoyment of 414 concert audiences. The group performs a wide variety of music, from Baroque and Classical, to Broadway musicals, popular, Sacred, Dixieland and jazz.

Availability: The Quartet prefers a Saturday afternoon or a Monday evening slot later in the month of January

Prep Time/Duties: Please have a staff person assigned to greet/interface with the performers and have the space set up 30 minutes prior to program start time.

Space/Equipment Needs: Community Room

Public Blurb: Enjoy a variety of musical pieces performed by the renowned local artists The Menlo Brass Quintet. The performance is sure to please the whole family.

Magic with Joe Caffall (Culture)	Click here to enter a date.	Start time:	Click here to enter a date.	Start time:	Community Room

Description: Joe Caffall is a Friend of the Edenvale Branch and was recommended by Edenvale staff. He is studying and practicing magic for over 30 years. His shows include color and surprise for preschoolers; a bit more mystery for older children, teens, and adults; and laughter, amazement, and fun for all. In his shows, everyday objects behave in uncommon ways. Audiences experience the impossible when familiar things like ropes, balloons, and playing cards act so strangely they won't believe their eyes. Lots of audience participation adds to the fun and excitement. This kind of show works well for library programs where there are children of different ages together with parents or caregivers. For library shows, he specifically points out at least one effect that can be learned from a book available at the library.

Public Blurb: Join us with the whole family for a fun and exciting show of magic with Joe Caffall. Children of all ages and their families are welcome!

Attendance Limits: none

Cost: $250 for a single booking or $200 per show for multiple bookings

Preparation Time/Duties: post flyer, promote event, welcome performer

Wings of the Hundred Viet Dance (Culture)	Click here to enter a date.	Start time:	Click here to enter a date.	Start time:	Community Room

Description: "Wings of the Hundred Viet Dance Company is a not-for-profit cultural group formed by Vietnamese youths." The group is composed of 20 dancers and they perform a folk tale. For more information about the group, please visit http://www.wingso100viet.org/home.htm **Please note they need a space at least 20' X 20' to do their performance, plus an isle through the audience for the dragon to perform (suitable only for branches with LARGE community rooms).**

Cost: $300–$500 donation.

Preparation Time/Duties: post flyer, promote event, welcome performer

Attendance Limits: For the whole family.

Notes:

Figure 8.4 (*Continued*)

For example, Brooke Ballard, teen librarian at San Antonio Public Library (SAPL) circulated teen program boxes. Her first version combined materials for two programs—movie night and craft night. They were neither rotated like storytime boxes nor selected from menus; instead, Brooke created catalog records for them in Millennium, SAPL's integrated library software. The records were suppressed from public view but staff could log into Millennium to place holds on the boxes, which could then be routed to branches along with customer-requested materials. When the box was shipped back to the main library, inventoried by teen staff, and checked in, another hold was triggered and the box was shipped off to the next branch on the list. Later, Brooke split up her boxes into separate movie and craft kits and began to circulate them herself, having branches sign up in advance. Routing slips such as the ones SJPL used for storytime boxes meant that each branch could ship their current box to the next location on the list. This caused inventory and routing problems, so now Brooke has switched to a hybrid version, where the boxes return to her department for replenishing before being shipped back out. Note that Brooke was willing to repeatedly modify this procedure to make it as easy for branch staff as possible, a critical factor in buy-in, especially when system-wide programming is not fully centralized (Brooke Ballard, email message to author, February 16, 2013).

If you're streamlining at a smaller library, you may not need centrally created menus, but you should still consider creating a monthly or yearly program plan. This could help you group certain types of programs together chronologically, so that you can promote them as a group, for example, Wellness Month or Celebrate Children's Books Week. You can also add notes about attendance numbers and prep time as well as what you did, when, and how, so that you can decide whether and when to repeat a program in the future.

9

Training and Marketing

Now that you've got your staff hired, menus filled out, and programs created, what's left? Two critical pieces remain for successful implementation of centralized programming. You have to train staff system-wide on how it all works so that programs are delivered seamlessly from the customer point of view. And you have to promote your programs successfully so customers know what you have to offer.

TRAINING

It's important to make your boxes, menus, and program instructions as user-friendly as possible in order to maintain the efficiency of your new model. Still, some training is likely to be needed. For example, are you expanding the range of staff who can present storytime? Will your computer classes be presented by teachers who are familiar with the technology but not with basic principles of education—or vice versa? How you conduct training will vary widely, depending on the scope of your changed programming model as well as the experience level of the staff presenting the programs. Still, there are some basic principles to keep in mind:

- Training should be hands-on whenever possible. Most people will learn best when they have the materials in their hands. It's quite different to watch a storytime demo and then go back to your branch than it is to watch a demo and then break into small groups to practice the techniques you've just learned.
- While training should overall be positive, more about what to do than what not to do, a "pitfalls to avoid" component can add humor to your training. If you're training on storytime boxes, for example, show the group how easy it is to angle the book you're reading up just enough that no one can see the pictures except you. If you're demonstrating how to teach an Intro to Computers class, point out use of jargon that will alienate the customers—if they're in a

beginning class, they won't understand phrases like "apply formatting" or "x out of the program."

- Whenever possible, have your front-line staff do the teaching. They are the experts on these particular topics, and they should have the opportunity to shine. An additional benefit is that you will earn buy-in from both the teachers and the students this way.

At San José Public Library (SJPL), the timing of our centralization kickoff coincided with severe municipal budget cuts that resulted in staff layoffs. One of the many ramifications was that librarian staff was reduced system-wide, and we no longer had the luxury of children's, teen, or adult specialists at every branch. Library administration issued the directive that all librarians were now expected to be able to provide storytime. Managers were also required to be able to pinch-hit for storytime. Since we had many adult services librarians and branch managers who had never done this before, we provided two levels of training on storytime boxes—one for experienced storytellers, who just needed to learn how to adapt the box components to their own audiences, and one more comprehensive, including a session on child development taught by our early education manager. The boxes actually made this particular transition easier, since new storytellers did not have to learn how to choose books, songs, and props, but they still had to learn how to structure a storytime, how to tailor box components to particular age groups, and more.

Not much training was needed aside from this piece. The box and virtual box programs were created by existing SJPL librarians who knew the front-line staff and included excellent instructions. We wanted the programming model to be self-evidently usable, much like a successful library website. We figured that if it needed a great deal of instruction, it was too complex in the first place.

MARKETING

Deciding who will promote your programs to the public depends on how much marketing is already centralized. If you're lucky enough to have a central marketing staff, how much program promotion have they done in the past, and how much was left up to individual branches?

At SJPL, at the time we implemented centralized programming, we had a central marketing and communications coordinator—one full-time employee with no support staff. Because of her limited time, only major system event series such as the Summer Reading Celebration and Silicon Valley Reads (our "big read" program) were promoted centrally. Each branch had a Facebook page from which local staff promoted their own events, and each created monthly printed program calendars as well. Branches were also responsible for making fliers for program promotion inside and outside the library, and for creating PowerPoint slides to be cycled on a large monitor each branch had installed near the checkout lines.

When the planning process for program centralization began, we wanted to centralize the marketing efforts as well. After all, now each branch would be working with the same pool of programs. It didn't make sense for each location offering our Making Musical Instruments class to create a flier from scratch when we could do that centrally. It would then be easy for us to turn those Word or Publisher documents into PowerPoint slides. Since we were already writing promotional blurbs for those fliers, it would be easy for us to paste those into branch program calendars, eliminating the need for branches to do that themselves.

This was a selling point for centralized programming in general. Branch staff had long hated the task of creating the monthly calendars. We'd hired a consultant a few years earlier who had made templates in Word for the calendars, but they were clunky and required great attention to detail—if, for example, you hit the Return key one too many times, the font would change. It was difficult to fit very much information into the tiny boxes provided. And beyond the template itself, branch staff who were making the calendars constantly had to revise them because a colleague would give them the wrong information for his programs, or because there were time or room changes after the deadline. Calendars were printed centrally via a copy shop with whom we contracted; but once branches received them, they often had to scratch out information that had changed since press time and write it in with a marker, resulting in a lot of staff time and an unattractive marketing tool.

In other words, branch staff were delighted to hear that with the advent of centralization, the central team would make program calendars for them. It helped staff buy into the concept. The central team, of course, was not as thrilled. Our support staff consisted of just one full-time clerk, who was talented and creative, but only worked 40 hours per week and had many other responsibilities. It proved impossible for her to make 19 calendars each month while still accomplishing her other duties. So, the calendar work was divided among all five of the staff on the team. Each librarian served as the liaison to a group of branches, so they made most of those calendars themselves, with the clerk taking one or two off the hands of each of them. This, of course, meant that the librarians were overworked, and could not meet their own deadlines. Eventually, we were able to obtain additional clerical help from another library department.

The next year, centralized programming responsibilities were moved to the reference and adult services department, where there were multiple clerical staff available to help out. I recommend that you have at least one full-time clerical staff member for each 10 branches if you intend to do marketing out of your own central team.

We used Evanced software to manage our event database. Evanced was supposed to be perfect for centralized programming because we would be able to enter an event title and description once and then set up multiple dates, times, and locations, but this belief proved false. Instead, our staff became experts at copying and pasting from one Evanced screen to the next, and then copying from Evanced and pasting into a Word document that would become a branch calendar. At the time, we had a traditional calendar format on the front of each calendar and a list of blurbs on the back. Each blurb had to be copied and pasted into the Word document.

We had also hoped that Evanced would be able to generate the calendar format portion of the monthly calendars, but this also turned out to be impossible. This was because the online version of the Evanced calendar displayed only one or two events per branch per day, with a "More" link to take users to the rest of the information. Obviously, this wouldn't work in print format. Eventually, the experts on our IT team were able to figure out a way to make Evanced display a full day's worth of programs on demand, and then, we could copy/paste into Word with a little less formatting required.

Online and external promotion was still left to the branches themselves. Each branch still had its own Facebook page, overseen in a general way by our digital services manager, but with content provided locally. Each event in Evanced had a "Share This" button that local staff could use to send events to its Facebook page, with added comments, if desired. Once the print calendars arrived at the branch, it was up to local staff to distribute them externally—to the local park district facility, on the bulletin board at a coffee shop, or wherever local staff knew they might find an audience. Fliers were not sent to the print shop, but posted on the library's intranet for downloading and printing by branch staff; promotional slides were also posted there for branch staff to download and pop into their PowerPoints.

SJPL did not offer online registration for programs, but Evanced does have that capability. Arapahoe (CO) Library District offers online registration via Evanced for their programs, as did Arlington Heights (IL) Memorial Library until recently. Arlington Heights has now developed an in-house Drupal-based solution to replace Evanced and improve upon it. Benefits include the ability for customers to view the programs for which they've registered from the My Account page of the website, alongside the books and other materials they have checked out.

If you work for a smaller library that is streamlining rather than centralizing, you can still use many of these techniques. You may not be able to afford an online calendar product, but you can use free social media tools to promote your programs. You could offer small incentives (A library-branded pencil? A $1 coupon for the Friends book sale?) to everyone who follows you on Twitter or likes you on Facebook. Try offering a slightly larger incentive ($5 gift card to a coffee shop) to the first 10 people who Instagram a photo from one of your programs.

Similarly, you can use templates to create fliers, even in a one-building library. Many of your staff probably do this already, merely "saving as" the last flier they created, then tweaking it for the new program they're promoting. Consider asking your best flier-maker to set up a template everyone can use; they can pop in the graphic of their choice; change the title, date, and time; print it out and be ready to go.

Your staff are trained, your programs are publicized . . . it's time to kick off!

10

Kickoff and Evaluation

KICKOFF

Kickoff is an exciting time! All your months of planning are now paying off. Your staff are revved up to present the first few programs they've created. Your branches are delighted they didn't have to create their own calendars and fliers. Your administration is proud of the hard work you've done.

You might be tempted to have a public celebration of your new model, the way you would on a branch anniversary or the opening of a new location, but this actually isn't such a good idea. This change is huge, but it's a behind-the-scenes change. Customers don't need to know that you've done this; if they think your programming has improved or gotten worse, they'll let you know. However, just as they don't need to know about organizational chart changes, city purchase order requirements, or what Z39.50 means, they don't need to know about this. (I once heard a speaker describe this as "don't show your corporate underpants"—a phrase I love.)

This may seem like antitransparency, but it's really a matter of keeping the customer experience cleaner. Your library visitors should be able to come in and ask any staff member a question and be led to an answer, not sent away with a terse "This is circulation and you want reference." Customers should have smooth, pleasant experiences without worrying about your internal staffing issues. Of course, if a customer asks why a different librarian than usual is doing your computer classes, you should answer honestly. Yet, rolling it out to customers as a whole is unnecessary at best, and counterproductive at worst.

FEEDBACK FROM CUSTOMERS

Ideally, your customers won't notice any changes, except perhaps improvements in quality at a location that was underperforming. However, wanting feedback on your programming model is different from wanting feedback on your individual programs. How have you evaluated programs in the past? With the aid of paper surveys handed out at each event or during selected classes? Was it through an online survey emailed to participants who registered? Or through an exit poll? By tracking increased or decreased attendance? Whatever you've done in the past, you should continue to do the same for the first year of centralized programming so that you can compare a full year of the new model to your previous year under the old model. Of course, you can add new measures, but you will want to compare apples to apples as well, so don't discard the old evaluations at the same time you eliminate the old model.

Wait, you haven't been collecting feedback on your existing programs? Okay, then, *now* is the perfect time to start. Think about what would work best within your new model. Do most people register for your programs online? Then an email survey would work well. Or is your library in a location with low computer literacy? Handing out paper surveys is a better idea, in such a case. In either case, make sure you have the survey translated into the appropriate languages. Even if the program is presented in English, listening to a performance in English is different from filling out a questionnaire in a language that isn't your first. Tracking attendance is also a good idea, though that is as much a measure of the day, time, and place of the program as of its quality.

WHAT YOU REALLY WANT TO TRACK

When you plan how to evaluate your programs, think about what you and your customers are trying to accomplish. Don't just ask people to rate the program on a scale of one to ten. What outcomes could the program have for your audience? How can you measure those?

Let's take toddler storytime as an example. Before you think of evaluation methods, think about what you actually want the program to achieve. What do you want storytime to accomplish? Do you want more parents to read to their children after attending storytime? Put that question on the form. Do you want to see increased picture book circulation during the hour before and after storytime? Keep track of your statistics, or put out extra copies of all the titles your storyteller reads that day, and see how fast those go out.

Christina Stoll, program services manager at Arlington Heights (IL) Memorial Library, revised her program evaluation surveys in mid-2013 to focus more on customers' stories about what the library could do for them. While previous surveys had asked such basic questions as "Rate the program's value to you" and "How did you hear about this program?" her revision included opportunities for customers to give real feedback. For example, one question asks what value a program had for the customer. The answer choices include the following:

- I learned something that will help me in school, at work, or home.
- I learned something that will help me solve a problem.
- I was entertained by the program.
- I made a connection with someone at the program.
- The program was not of value to me.

After the question, Christina asked the customer to explain how the program had an impact on his life, with space to elaborate the ideas. She included optional blanks for the customer's name and contact information in case the library wanted to contact him about his experience, either to try to repair a negative impression or to share his story in promotional efforts to illustrate how the library adds value to its customers' lives. Since the survey was, at press time, only recently rolled out, it's too soon to have data about how the survey has helped, but Christina should have a better understanding of what programs to offer and about how to promote them. She can also pass along especially memorable feedback to the director of communications and marketing, who can then use them as testimonials on the library's website or newsletter (Christina Stoll, in discussion with the author, June 7, 2013).

FEEDBACK FROM STAFF

As mentioned in Chapter 2, it's nearly impossible to overcommunicate with staff. This doesn't just mean filling inboxes and meeting agendas with one-way communication, but to hear from front-line staff about how the model is progressing, as well as their input on individual programs they've observed or presented.

A key part of the role of the central unit is to make it easy for staff to provide feedback. The unit's manager should be available through the usual methods—email, phone, and walk-in—so that staff can contact her spontaneously. You could also assign each branch or unit a liaison on your central team so front-line staff always have someone to call first with a problem.

It's also a good idea to set up methods for central staff and the project team to receive feedback on a regular basis. At San José Public Library (SJPL), we sent out a monthly Zoomerang (now SurveyMonkey) questionnaire asking staff to rate each of our programs on a four-point scale—excellent, good, fair, or poor. After getting feedback on the survey itself, after the first month, we asked staff to rate each program on two scales—one for quality, the other for popularity and relevance to the community (see Appendix). We continued to add other questions as time went on, such as the following:

- Does storytime prep take more time, less time, or about the same as it did before centralized programming?
- Were there any programs offered this month that appealed to a different age group than the one we had in mind?
- Do you have any ideas for improving the program menu?
- What question aren't we asking that we should ask?

For a detailed example of a survey, please refer to the Appendix.

Staff were required to fill out the surveys as a branch or unit, one response per location. We received a lot of useful feedback on individual programs, particularly on paid presenters or partner-produced programs that the central team was not there to see in person. We also had the opportunity to witness the "time heals all wounds" maxim of change management, as approval ratings for our storytime boxes climbed month after month—for the same boxes.

Yes, you will see more negative feedback than you'd like at first, much of which is aimed at the concept rather than at the specific topic or event about which you're asking. For this reason, it's advisable to have open-ended questions to elicit complete thoughts from the staff; it's easier for employees to be generically critical when they can simply check boxes than it is when they need to write it out themselves.

In his book *Adult Programs in the Library,* Brett W. Lear (2013, 177–179) suggests having the staff who present a program fill out a one-page evaluation immediately after each program, in addition to the customer evaluations. He uses a paper form that has two sections. The top one is filled out by the central team, listing the program's goals (e.g., target audience), and quantifying the work they've put in and the promotion done by the marketing department. The bottom half is filled out by the presenting staff member, who answers questions about attendance, branch resources used, local publicity done, and general comments from both the audience and the staff member. A sample evaluation form loosely based on Lear's is included here as Figure 10.1.

In addition to all of the above, our central team sought feedback on our storytime boxes by starting individual discussion boards on our intranet site, one per box. The hope was that branch staff would not only provide feedback on the individual boxes, but also let us know via the discussion boards when a box was missing a toy or running out of stickers. We even hoped that branch librarians would use the boards to talk about the creative ways in which they'd used the box contents. Unfortunately, this didn't happen. We heard about the boxes in other ways, such as email and via

PROGRAM EVALUATION SAMPLE

Thank you for attending library programs. So that we can continue to meet the community's needs, please take a few minutes to fill out this survey. You can also provide feedback directly to the Programs Coordinator (408-555-5555/programs@yourlibrary.org).

Today's date _____

Which program did you attend today? _____

How often do you attend library programs?

☑ Every week
☑ Every month
☑ Several times per year
☑ Once per year or less
☑ This is my first time attending a library program

Would you recommend this program to others? If so, to whom?

_____

What did you gain from today's program? Check all that apply.

☑ I learned new information I can use in my life
☑ I learned new theoretical information
☑ I solved a problem
☑ I made a connection with someone
☑ I learned more about the library and its resources
☑ I didn't gain anything

How could we improve this program?

_____

What other programs would you be interested in seeing at the library?

_____

Would you like to sign up for our email newsletter announcing library programs and services? If so, please provide your email address.

_____

Thank you for taking the time to help improve library programming.

Figure 10.1   Sample program evaluation form

liaisons, but understandably, the bulletin boards were just not a priority for our busy branch staff. Without being required by administration or their managers to provide feedback at this level, and without calendar or email reminders, this step fell by the wayside.

As you move along through your project timeline, and staff adjust to the centralized model, try to set up ways to encourage front-line staff to develop programs that can then be used centrally. To make this more fun, consider using Pinterest to pin ideas for all to see. Amy Mather, programs & lifelong learning manager at Omaha Public Library, uses Pinterest and Socialcast to share programming ideas with her colleagues. She sets up pinboards by topics such as Summer Reading or Money Smart Week (Amy Mather, email message to author, April 24, 2013).

META-FEEDBACK

As you roll out your streamlined or centralized programming, it's important for you to get continual feedback, both detailed and big-picture, from front-line staff as well as from managers. As manager of the central team at SJPL, I ran a meta-feedback session at one of our managerial meetings. I broke up the managers into small groups and asked questions about how they preferred to give programming feedback, whom it should come from (directly from staff or funneled through managers), and how they thought our team had done at listening to and incorporating feedback. On each questionnaire sheet, a "Parking Lot" section was included—that is, a blank area for staff to comment on other concerns. I knew that the temptation to comment on individual programs and the overall concept, rather than specifically on feedback, would be present, and these blank spaces provided a spot where such comments could be "parked" for discussion at a later time.

No matter the size of your library or the scope of your project, evaluation of your programming is essential. Collecting feedback can be exhausting emotionally (no one likes negative reviews!) and take up time that you may feel could be better spent elsewhere. Do it anyway! Remember, your public library exists to serve your community, and you can only do that well if you know which elements of service are popular and which are not.

Congratulations on finishing this book! Maybe you've been working on each piece along the way, or maybe you read it all before getting started to see what's involved. Either way, it's time to dive in. Experiment and tweak to match your library's community, size, structure, current state, and goals for the future. Take this book's chapters as guidelines, recommendations, and stories about how a few libraries have managed the move to centralized or streamlined programming, but remember there are as many ways to do this as there are public libraries. You can chart your own course. I would love to hear from libraries that have begun the process; we can learn from each other by sharing our stories. Good luck, and happy streamlining!

Appendix

San José Public Library
Staff Program Survey

*1. What location are you from?

O Almaden
O Alum Rock
O Alviso
O Biblioteca Latinoamericana
O Berryessa
O Cambrian
O Edenvale
O Evergreen
O East Branch
O Hillview

O Joyce Ellington
O King
O Pearl Avenue
O Rose Garden
O Santa Teresa
O Tully
O Vineland
O West Valley
O Willow Glen

2. How would you rate the English-language storytime boxes you used in May?

Poor	Fair	Good	Excellent	N/A
O	O	O	O	O

3. How would you rate the Spanish-language storytime boxes you used in May?

Poor	Fair	Good	Excellent	N/A
O	O	O	O	O

© San José Public Library

From *Streamlined Library Programming: How to Improve Services and Cut Costs* by Daisy Porter-Reynolds. Santa Barbara, CA: Libraries Unlimited. Copyright © 2014.

4. **In May, did you spend more time, less time, or about the same amount of time prepping for storytime than you did prior to centralized programming?**

○ We spent more time in May
○ We spent less time in May
○ About the same
○ Other, please specify

5. **In May, which elements of the storytime boxes did you use? Please choose all that apply.**

☐ Books for preschoolers
☐ Books for toddlers
☐ Music CD
☐ Flannelboards
☐ Puppets, toys, etc.
☐ Coloring sheets
☐ Lyric sheets
☐ Stickers
☐ Online supplements on SharePoint
☐ Other, please specify

6. **Paid Presenter: Chiquy Boom**

1 = poor, 2 = fair, 3 = good, 4 = excellent, n/a

	1	2	3	4	N/A
Popularity, attendance, meeting community needs	○	○	○	○	○
Quality, ease of use, quality of materials and presenter	○	○	○	○	○

Additional Comments:

7. Paid Presenter: Victor Hugo Sanchez

1 = poor, 2 = fair, 3 = good, 4 = excellent, n/a

	1	2	3	4	N/A
Popularity, attendance, meeting community needs	O	O	O	O	O
Quality, ease of use, quality of materials and presenter	O	O	O	O	O

Additional Comments:

8. Paid Presenter: Art n Motion

1 = poor, 2 = fair, 3 = good, 4 = excellent, n/a

	1	2	3	4	N/A
Popularity, attendance, meeting community needs	O	O	O	O	O
Quality, ease of use, quality of materials and presenter	O	O	O	O	O

Additional Comments:

9. Paid Presenter: Baby Sign Language

1 = poor, 2 = fair, 3 = good, 4 = excellent, n/a

	1	2	3	4	N/A
Popularity, attendance, meeting community needs	O	O	O	O	O
Quality, ease of use, quality of materials and presenter	O	O	O	O	O

Additional Comments:

10. Paid Presenter: Bike to Work Day Energizer Station

1 = poor, 2 = fair, 3 = good, 4 = excellent, n/a

	1	2	3	4	N/A
Popularity, attendance, meeting community needs	O	O	O	O	O
Quality, ease of use, quality of materials and presenter	O	O	O	O	O

Additional Comments:

---

11. Paid Presenter: B. J. King on Job Searching

1 = poor, 2 = fair, 3 = good, 4 = excellent, n/a

	1	2	3	4	N/A
Popularity, attendance, meeting community needs	O	O	O	O	O
Quality, ease of use, quality of materials and presenter	O	O	O	O	O

Additional Comments:

---

12. Paid Presenter: Greeting Card Creations

1 = poor, 2 = fair, 3 = good, 4 = excellent, n/a

	1	2	3	4	N/A
Popularity, attendance, meeting community needs	O	O	O	O	O
Quality, ease of use, quality of materials and presenter	O	O	O	O	O

Additional Comments:

---

13. Paid Presenter: Grupo Folklorico Los Laureles

1 = poor, 2 = fair, 3 = good, 4 = excellent, n/a

	1	2	3	4	N/A
Popularity, attendance, meeting community needs	O	O	O	O	O
Quality, ease of use, quality of materials and presenter	O	O	O	O	O

Additional Comments:

14. Paid Presenter: Physics All Around You

1 = poor, 2 = fair, 3 = good, 4 = excellent, n/a

	1	2	3	4	N/A
Popularity, attendance, meeting community needs	O	O	O	O	O
Quality, ease of use, quality of materials and presenter	O	O	O	O	O

Additional Comments:

15. Paid Presenter: Traveling Reptile Program

1 = poor, 2 = fair, 3 = good, 4 = excellent, n/a

	1	2	3	4	N/A
Popularity, attendance, meeting community needs	O	O	O	O	O
Quality, ease of use, quality of materials and presenter	O	O	O	O	O

Additional Comments:

16. Paid Presenter: Science with Children's Discovery Museum

1 = poor, 2 = fair, 3 = good, 4 = excellent, n/a

	1	2	3	4	N/A
Popularity, attendance, meeting community needs	O	O	O	O	O
Quality, ease of use, quality of materials and presenter	O	O	O	O	O

Additional Comments:

---

17. UPS Program: Author Visit from Julie Riera Matsushima

1 = poor, 2 = fair, 3 = good, 4 = excellent, n/a

	1	2	3	4	N/A
Popularity, attendance, meeting community needs	O	O	O	O	O
Quality, ease of use, quality of materials and presenter	O	O	O	O	O

Additional Comments:

---

18. UPS Program: Before You Buy: New Car

1 = poor, 2 = fair, 3 = good, 4 = excellent, n/a

	1	2	3	4	N/A
Popularity, attendance, meeting community needs	O	O	O	O	O
Quality, ease of use, quality of materials and presenter	O	O	O	O	O

Additional Comments:

---

19. UPS Program: Chronic Disease Self-Management

1 = poor, 2 = fair, 3 = good, 4 = excellent, n/a

	1	2	3	4	N/A
Popularity, attendance, meeting community needs	O	O	O	O	O
Quality, ease of use, quality of materials and presenter	O	O	O	O	O

Additional Comments:

_____

20. UPS Program: Disaster Prep from City of San José

1 = poor, 2 = fair, 3 = good, 4 = excellent, n/a

	1	2	3	4	N/A
Popularity, attendance, meeting community needs	O	O	O	O	O
Quality, ease of use, quality of materials and presenter	O	O	O	O	O

Additional Comments:

_____

21. UPS Program: Disaster Prep from Red Cross

1 = poor, 2 = fair, 3 = good, 4 = excellent, n/a

	1	2	3	4	N/A
Popularity, attendance, meeting community needs	O	O	O	O	O
Quality, ease of use, quality of materials and presenter	O	O	O	O	O

Additional Comments:

_____

22. UPS Program: Simple Steps to Going Green

1 = poor, 2 = fair, 3 = good, 4 = excellent, n/a

	1	2	3	4	N/A
Popularity, attendance, meeting community needs	O	O	O	O	O
Quality, ease of use, quality of materials and presenter	O	O	O	O	O

Additional Comments:

---

23. UPS Program: Go Wild! Kids' Nature Program

1 = poor, 2 = fair, 3 = good, 4 = excellent, n/a

	1	2	3	4	N/A
Popularity, attendance, meeting community needs	O	O	O	O	O
Quality, ease of use, quality of materials and presenter	O	O	O	O	O

Additional Comments:

---

24. UPS Program: Introduction to Twitter

1 = poor, 2 = fair, 3 = good, 4 = excellent, n/a

	1	2	3	4	N/A
Popularity, attendance, meeting community needs	O	O	O	O	O
Quality, ease of use, quality of materials and presenter	O	O	O	O	O

Additional Comments:

---

25. UPS Program: Math Fun: Look Around

1 = poor, 2 = fair, 3 = good, 4 = excellent, n/a

	1	2	3	4	N/A
Popularity, attendance, meeting community needs	O	O	O	O	O
Quality, ease of use, quality of materials and presenter	O	O	O	O	O

Additional Comments:

26. UPS Program: Mission Chamber Orchestra

1 = poor, 2 = fair, 3 = good, 4 = excellent, n/a

	1	2	3	4	N/A
Popularity, attendance, meeting community needs	O	O	O	O	O
Quality, ease of use, quality of materials and presenter	O	O	O	O	O

Additional Comments:

27. UPS Program: Piñata Craft and Story

1 = poor, 2 = fair, 3 = good, 4 = excellent, n/a

	1	2	3	4	N/A
Popularity, attendance, meeting community needs	O	O	O	O	O
Quality, ease of use, quality of materials and presenter	O	O	O	O	O

Additional Comments:

28. UPS Program: Play and Learn: Making Play-Doh

1 = poor, 2 = fair, 3 = good, 4 = excellent, n/a

	1	2	3	4	N/A
Popularity, attendance, meeting community needs	O	O	O	O	O
Quality, ease of use, quality of materials and presenter	O	O	O	O	O

Additional Comments:

---

29. UPS Program: Social Security Online Application Assistance

1 = poor, 2 = fair, 3 = good, 4 = excellent, n/a

	1	2	3	4	N/A
Popularity, attendance, meeting community needs	O	O	O	O	O
Quality, ease of use, quality of materials and presenter	O	O	O	O	O

Additional Comments:

---

30. UPS Program: Preparing for the Zombie Apocalypse

1 = poor, 2 = fair, 3 = good, 4 = excellent, n/a

	1	2	3	4	N/A
Popularity, attendance, meeting community needs	O	O	O	O	O
Quality, ease of use, quality of materials and presenter	O	O	O	O	O

Additional Comments:

---

31. Program in a Box: Before You Buy (series)

1 = poor, 2 = fair, 3 = good, 4 = excellent, n/a

	1	2	3	4	N/A
Popularity, attendance, meeting community needs	O	O	O	O	O
Quality, ease of use, quality of materials and presenter	O	O	O	O	O

Additional Comments:

32. Program in a Box: Branch Birthday Party

1 = poor, 2 = fair, 3 = good, 4 = excellent, n/a

	1	2	3	4	N/A
Popularity, attendance, meeting community needs	O	O	O	O	O
Quality, ease of use, quality of materials and presenter	O	O	O	O	O

Additional Comments:

33. Program in a Box: Book Adventures

1 = poor, 2 = fair, 3 = good, 4 = excellent, n/a

	1	2	3	4	N/A
Popularity, attendance, meeting community needs	O	O	O	O	O
Quality, ease of use, quality of materials and presenter	O	O	O	O	O

Additional Comments:

34. Program in a Box: Sports & News Online

1 = poor, 2 = fair, 3 = good, 4 = excellent, n/a

	1	2	3	4	N/A
Popularity, attendance, meeting community needs	O	O	O	O	O
Quality, ease of use, quality of materials and presenter	O	O	O	O	O

Additional Comments:

_____

35. Program in a Box: Calendar Bingo

1 = poor, 2 = fair, 3 = good, 4 = excellent, n/a

	1	2	3	4	N/A
Popularity, attendance, meeting community needs	O	O	O	O	O
Quality, ease of use, quality of materials and presenter	O	O	O	O	O

Additional Comments:

_____

36. Program in a Box: Citizenship Study Group

1 = poor, 2 = fair, 3 = good, 4 = excellent, n/a

	1	2	3	4	N/A
Popularity, attendance, meeting community needs	O	O	O	O	O
Quality, ease of use, quality of materials and presenter	O	O	O	O	O

Additional Comments:

_____

37. Program in a Box: Computer Basics series

1 = poor, 2 = fair, 3 = good, 4 = excellent, n/a

	1	2	3	4	N/A
Popularity, attendance, meeting community needs	O	O	O	O	O
Quality, ease of use, quality of materials and presenter	O	O	O	O	O

Additional Comments:

---

38. Program in a Box: Reading Readiness in English

1 = poor, 2 = fair, 3 = good, 4 = excellent, n/a

	1	2	3	4	N/A
Popularity, attendance, meeting community needs	O	O	O	O	O
Quality, ease of use, quality of materials and presenter	O	O	O	O	O

Additional Comments:

---

39. Program in a Box: Reading Readiness in Spanish

1 = poor, 2 = fair, 3 = good, 4 = excellent, n/a

	1	2	3	4	N/A
Popularity, attendance, meeting community needs	O	O	O	O	O
Quality, ease of use, quality of materials and presenter	O	O	O	O	O

Additional Comments:

40. Program in a Box: Reading Readiness in Mandarin

1 = poor, 2 = fair, 3 = good, 4 = excellent, n/a

	1	2	3	4	N/A
Popularity, attendance, meeting community needs	O	O	O	O	O
Quality, ease of use, quality of materials and presenter	O	O	O	O	O

Additional Comments:

---

41. Program in a Box: Wii Tournament

1 = poor, 2 = fair, 3 = good, 4 = excellent, n/a

	1	2	3	4	N/A
Popularity, attendance, meeting community needs	O	O	O	O	O
Quality, ease of use, quality of materials and presenter	O	O	O	O	O

Additional Comments:

---

42. Program in a Box: Music and Movement

1 = poor, 2 = fair, 3 = good, 4 = excellent, n/a

	1	2	3	4	N/A
Popularity, attendance, meeting community needs	O	O	O	O	O
Quality, ease of use, quality of materials and presenter	O	O	O	O	O

Additional Comments:

---

43. Program in a Box: Snack Smart

1 = poor, 2 = fair, 3 = good, 4 = excellent, n/a

	1	2	3	4	N/A
Popularity, attendance, meeting community needs	O	O	O	O	O
Quality, ease of use, quality of materials and presenter	O	O	O	O	O

Additional Comments:

_____

44. Program in a Box: Intro to Facebook

1 = poor, 2 = fair, 3 = good, 4 = excellent, n/a

	1	2	3	4	N/A
Popularity, attendance, meeting community needs	O	O	O	O	O
Quality, ease of use, quality of materials and presenter	O	O	O	O	O

Additional Comments:

_____

45. Program in a Box: Parent/Child Computer Class series

1 = poor, 2 = fair, 3 = good, 4 = excellent, n/a

	1	2	3	4	N/A
Popularity, attendance, meeting community needs	O	O	O	O	O
Quality, ease of use, quality of materials and presenter	O	O	O	O	O

Additional Comments:

_____

46. Program in a Box: Putting Your Photos Online

1 = poor, 2 = fair, 3 = good, 4 = excellent, n/a

	1	2	3	4	N/A
Popularity, attendance, meeting community needs	O	O	O	O	O
Quality, ease of use, quality of materials and presenter	O	O	O	O	O

Additional Comments:

47. Program in a Box: Mixing in Math series

1 = poor, 2 = fair, 3 = good, 4 = excellent, n/a

	1	2	3	4	N/A
Popularity, attendance, meeting community needs	O	O	O	O	O
Quality, ease of use, quality of materials and presenter	O	O	O	O	O

Additional Comments:

48. Program in a Box: Mother's Day Storytime with Craft

1 = poor, 2 = fair, 3 = good, 4 = excellent, n/a

	1	2	3	4	N/A
Popularity, attendance, meeting community needs	O	O	O	O	O
Quality, ease of use, quality of materials and presenter	O	O	O	O	O

Additional Comments:

49. Program in a Box: Health Information Online

1 = poor, 2 = fair, 3 = good, 4 = excellent, n/a

	1	2	3	4	N/A
Popularity, attendance, meeting community needs	○	○	○	○	○
Quality, ease of use, quality of materials and presenter	○	○	○	○	○

Additional Comments:

50. Program in a Box: Healthy Habits

1 = poor, 2 = fair, 3 = good, 4 = excellent, n/a

	1	2	3	4	N/A
Popularity, attendance, meeting community needs	○	○	○	○	○
Quality, ease of use, quality of materials and presenter	○	○	○	○	○

Additional Comments:

51. Program in a Box: Teen Craft 1: Mother's Day Cards

1 = poor, 2 = fair, 3 = good, 4 = excellent, n/a

	1	2	3	4	N/A
Popularity, attendance, meeting community needs	○	○	○	○	○
Quality, ease of use, quality of materials and presenter	○	○	○	○	○

Additional Comments:

52. Program in a Box: Teen Craft 2: Duct Tape

1 = poor, 2 = fair, 3 = good, 4 = excellent, n/a

	1	2	3	4	N/A
Popularity, attendance, meeting community needs	O	O	O	O	O
Quality, ease of use, quality of materials and presenter	O	O	O	O	O

Additional Comments:

_____

53. Program in a Box: Teen Craft 3: Candle Holders

1 = poor, 2 = fair, 3 = good, 4 = excellent, n/a

	1	2	3	4	N/A
Popularity, attendance, meeting community needs	O	O	O	O	O
Quality, ease of use, quality of materials and presenter	O	O	O	O	O

Additional Comments:

_____

54. Did you have any programs that appealed to an age group different than the one we marketed to? For example, did teens come to Teen Crafts, or did you get younger children?

55. Are there any types of programs or specific presenters you'd like to see on the menu in coming months?

56. Do you have any suggestions for making the menu easier to use?

57. What questions should we ask that we're not asking?

58. How do you and your customers like the new calendar format, promoting four big programs on the back rather than individual blurbs?

59. Any final comments?

Bibliography

Bowen, Johanna, et al. "Final Task Force Report to the Library Joint Powers Board on Financially Sustainable Service Models for the Santa Cruz Public Libraries." January 30, 2011, accessed April 14, 2013, http://www.santacruzpl.org/media/pdf/task_force/data/task_force_final_rpt.pdf.

Chase's Calendar of Events. Chicago: Contemporary Books, 1994–.

Crowther, Janet L., and Barry Trott. *Partnering with Purpose: A Guide to Strategic Partnership Development for Libraries and Other Organizations.* Santa Barbara, CA: Libraries Unlimited, 2004.

Diamant-Cohen, Betsy, ed. *Children's Services: Partnerships for Success.* Chicago: ALA Editions, 2010.

Grover, Robert J., Roger C. Greer, and John Agada. *Assessing Information Needs: Managing Transformative Library Services.* Santa Barbara, CA: Libraries Unlimited, 2010.

Institute of Museum and Library Services. *Public Libraries in the United States Survey: Fiscal Year 2010.* Washington, DC: IMLS, January 2013.

Lear, Brett W. *Adult Programs in the Library, Second Edition.* Chicago: American Library Association, 2013.

Nelson, Jennifer, and Keith Braafladt. *Technology and Literacy: 21st Century Library Programming for Children & Teens.* Chicago: American Library Association, 2012. Used with permission of the American Library Association.

Pritchett, Price. *Resistance: Moving Beyond the Barriers to Change: A Handbook for People Who Make Things Happen.* Dallas: Pritchett & Associates, Inc., 1996.

Index

About the Author

DAISY PORTER-REYNOLDS is Deputy Director at Arlington Heights (IL) Memorial Library, where she oversees library public services. Previously, she was Manager of Innovation at San José (CA) Public Library. Daisy has presented extensively on centralized programming, library service models, and teen literature.